CON AULD'S
LETTERS TO A CAUSEWAY
COAST MILL HOUSE

Limited Publication

Published by Con Auld
"The Braddan"
Port Braddan
Co. Antrim BT57 8TA
© Con Auld

Secretarial and Word Processing by CopyCats
537 Antrim Road, Belfast BT15 3BU
Printed by Spectator & Chronicle Newspaper Group
Balloo Link Bangor BT19 7HJ
ISBN No. 0.9542274-2.5
2004

BY THE SAME AUTHOR:

HOLYWOOD CO. DOWN THEN AND NOW – (2002)
I.S.B.N. 0-9542274-0-9

FORGOTTEN HOUSES OF HOLYWOOD, CO. DOWN – (2003)
I.S.B.N. 0-9542274-1-7

TITLES IN PREPARATION:

BUTTONS FOR THE PRIMATE
CHARACTERS OF HOLYWOOD CO. DOWN
FORGOTTEN HOUSES OF EAST BELFAST
HOLIDAY LETTERS FROM AN IRISH BANKER
HOLYWOOD INHERITANCE

I should like to record special appreciation to the four Ulster Artists
whose fine work is reproduced as exactly as possible.

To James McIntyre for St. Gobhan's Church

To (the late) Donald McPherson for 'Templastragh Farm' and 'Dunluce Castle'

To (the late) Eamon F. Murphy for 'Port Braddan in 1979'

To Robert G. Sellars for 'Port Braddan in the 1950's'.

LETTERS TO A CAUSEWAY COAST MILL

CONTENTS

BY WAY OF INTRODUCTION ......

Welcome to the Giant's Causeway Coast of County Antrim and to the Mill House at Port Braddan.

Alphon Daudet's *'Lettres De Mon Moulin'* was my favourite book in faraway school days. It is a collection of short stories, depicting country life in Provence, his birthplace. Daudet wrote his tales as letters from the windmill in which he lived. They are sympathetic character portrayals with vivid presentations of amusing incidents.

Many years after fifth form French classes in Belfast Royal Academy, I bought the former watermill at Port Braddan and converted the property into a Causeway Coast cottage. I soon found that the surrounding area was a living Irish history book, peopled with fascinating characters – very similar to Daudet's Provence.

This little book brings together eighteen letters written pseudonymously. They paint a picture of the saga of the Causeway Coast from Mesolithic times to the twenty first century.

The correspondents who walk through the pages, in former days travelled the roads and lanes of North Antrim. I have attempted to accommodate the mode of expression to the character of the letter writer. I hope the individuals, themselves, will shine through the various styles of writing. If nothing else, the letters confirm that fact is more interesting than fiction!

I am sure you will find special favourites among the major contributors, as you enjoy their lifestyles. To me the most memorable are the minor players. Those which come to mind are: dear old governess Hodgson of Dundarave, who was killed when stepping off a red London omnibus; poor William of Dunseverick, killed in a threshing machine at harvest time, or the child who played with little seashells at the Port Braddan cave, thousands of years ago!

I hope you will enjoy the letters and pencil sketches. Perhaps, you will go to see the places mentioned in the text; all await your visit. Do come to St. Gobban's Church and tell me your thoughts and corrections for the book. Maybe, like myself, you will seize the opportunity to restore an old cottage in the area and become a sojourner with the kindly people of the Causeway Coast, whose heritage is unrivalled and whose hospitality is legendary.

Con Auld

"The Braddan"
Port Braddan
2004.

I. THE ARCHAEOLOGIST'S LETTER

A. McL May. Port Braddan c. 7000 BC.

Greetings to your mill from one who has been an honorary Port Braddaner. That was for five short years, which were among the most enjoyable and interesting of my life.

I came to Port Braddan in 1931 to visit John McKay, your predecessor in the mill property and owner of the Port Braddan cave. We enjoyed a long morning of conversation. Later Martha McKay gave us one of her delicious salmon luncheons, for which she is famous. This culinary expertise I was soon to discover from frequent visits to the McKay boarding house.

John McKay told me the story of a cave he owned below Rossmore, the headland after which he had named the guest house. We walked along the path at the foot of the basalt cliff to take a first look at the cave, which was to be an excavation site from the Christmas vacation of 1935 until war broke out in 1939.

The river, which once turned your mill wheel, delves into the geological fault dividing the white limestone cliffs from the black basalt heights. There are many caves in the soluable limestone but the Port Braddan cave stretches sixty-two feet into the solid basalt. Perhaps its subterranean incision goes further. A local tale tells how two boys drove a frightened fox into the cave, which eventually emerged from a sink hole at Templastragh village – some half mile inland.

The Ministry of Finance offered grant aid for my archaeological project under the unemployment relief scheme and excavation commenced in 1935. Each day the team of workers passed the stack rock at the foot of Rossmore and came through the arch under Gid Point. Nature created this curiosity through erosion of the back wall of a cavern which formerly faced White Park Bay. Steps descend from the arch to the little rockbound cove unto which Port Braddan cave opens.

At some time a second entry into the cove had been made by breaking through part of the rock face division from Portacallan. Today hikers on the coastal path of the Ulster Way walk unhindered past the cave, in former days the cove was completely secluded as approach from sea or land was extremely difficult. This was before the arch and the Portacallan gate were opened.[1]

Portacallan has its own interest. To its high cliffs John McKay had diverted the Templastragh river from the Port Braddan ravine, with the intention of building a hydro-electric plant. The little bay is strewn with flint chips – perhaps the residents of our cave came here to make tools, using flint nodules from the White Park cliffs. From Portacallan, Islay and the Mull of Kintyre glisten on the far horizon, sending invitations to explore the mainland, far across the waters with its strange sounding names. From Portacallan a wrack (kelp) lane clings its winding way up the cliff to the old church with twin graveyards and seaweed hungry fields.

In the 1830 Ordnance Survey, Lieutenant Thomas Hore of the Royal Engineers, did not give

Port Braddan. Linoprint 12" x 16". R. G. Sellar.

a name to the cave cove hidden between Gid Point and Portacallan. However "Skull Cave" was his description of our excavation site. *"Skull cave is so called in consequence of several skulls and other bones having been found there at some former period, and supposed to be those of persons who took refuge in the cave during the 1641 war, but who were discovered and murdered in the place. Opposite the cave is a deep pit in the edge of the sea called the Murder Hole, and where it is said that numbers of persons had been thrown into at the above period. The cave was for years occupied as a smuggling concern"*. Little did the good Lieutenant Hore know that a century after the first ordnance survey, our excavation would find skulls and bones of much earlier times!

When we started work, we found a seven feet high bank of soil and stones, almost blocking the cave entrance. Most of this had fallen from the field above the cliff. We cut a passage, eight feet wide and six feet deep through this obstacle. Soon we uncovered a stone wall curving beyond the cave mouth. The wall had an opening, three feet wide, into the cave itself.

When we got into the cave, we saw the roof arching upwards for eighteen feet, then downwards for eighteen feet, and extending for sixty six feet at a width of about twenty five feet. We found *"recent additions,"* platforms stretching along each wall at the latest habitation level. The platforms provided dry accommodation areas for the residents, or for the smugglers, to which Lieutenant Hore referred!

The first family to enjoy the security of the Port Braddan cave arrived after the land had surged up to form a raised beach. The last ice sheets melted about ten millennia ago, causing the sea level to fluctuate from 100 to 300 feet and creating the raised

beaches of the present day. To these beaches came the first inhabitants of Ireland. The Mesolithic sea-food eaters. Their stature was a mere five feet, they were skilled makers of microliths, flint tools which they hafted with wood or bone. Probably they had learned how to make dug-out canoes, certainly the little people of the Port Braddan cave would have required such a form of transport. Perhaps they had discovered how to train wild dogs as our best friends.[2] These clever people were the first residents of Port Braddan. We shall never know how they found our cave, but they left many evidences of occupation.

As archaeologicals, we had to devise a viable plan for excavation of the site. Instead of cutting

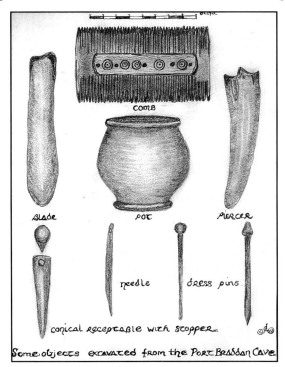

COMB

BLADE   POT   PIERCER

needle   dress pins

conical receptacle with stopper

Some objects excavated from the Port Braddan Cave

sections through the cave floor for immediate examination, we decided to carry outside the entire accumulation of material for exhustive research in the clear light of day. We excavated the site to the place where early occupation ceased.

We selected a convenient digging point ten feet inside the cave, which afforded a work face seven feet in height. For the sake of compiling an easily understandable record of the items which were uncovered, we divided the work-face into seven layers of twelve inches each above the beach. The accumulation below the beach we called *"Level One"*. This gave us a work site of eight levels.

The first cave dwellers left the gravel beach as clean as the light coloured pig bones we found upon it. They were skilled fireplace builders, having discovered the great gift of the gods, as did **Prometheus. Time taught them that superior** calorific value came from careful draught control. I shall return to the subject of fireplaces when we come to the higher levels of excavation.

Still on the beach, we found molluscs in profusion.[3] It seems someone had been playing games with these limpet shells, building up little conical towers, shell placed inside shell! Perhaps the little castles were the remains of childrens' games, undisturbed for thousands of years, now seeing the daylight of the twentieth century!

Now let me tell you in brief what we unearthed as we excavated the seven feet section face, in twelve inch division levels. The section immediately above the beach disclosed disintegrated shells, black soil, charcoal and dark coloured bones. The third section yielded flints, human remains and a fascinating little bone receptacle.

Section four gave us pottery sherds, human bones; clay, dark soil, red ash and a wide-spread scattering of grain seeds. Section five disclosed more sherds, needles, pins and a broken bone comb. At section six iron particles, sherds and a stone figurine saw the light of day. Section seven was a layer of limpets. Finally we found cobbles spread between the wall platforms. The floor at this point yielded up a rusty bayonet and a pistol barrel.

The Port Braddan cave dwellers appear to have enjoyed many of life's essentials. Good spring-well water was available at the mouth of the cave. Hunting skills provided sea food and animals for meat and skin clothing. Heat, light and defence came from ever burning fires.

I have mentioned the many Mesolithic age triple stone fireplaces on the original beach level, all built at the angle of maximum draught flow. Most of the fireplaces were built close to the entrance. A large number of small fireplaces appear to have been more efficient than a few large fires. This probably increased heat level inside the cave, provided smoke control and offered a selection of cooking hobs which could be kept at different temperatures.[4].

Of course, we experimented with fires in the cave itself, lighting them in various places. We found the smoke from them did not bother us over much, unless a violent north wind was storming into the cave! Smoke from the fires rose to the roof and drifted to the entrance, where it was drawn up the cliff face. The troublesome effect of the smoke was to flush out roof spiders; their silken escape lines to the floor annoyed us much more than the smoke. I wonder did the smart little cave dwellers discover the many uses of spiders' webs?

Two fireplaces require special mention. One had a neatly fitted square paved hearth. The other was three feet long and over two feet high, it was built with large angular stones and equipped with excellent hobs around the fire. It seems our ancestors *"rid the ashes"* by brushing them across the floor into heaps against the cave walls. In one place ash could be traced over the entire width of the cave, in another place we counted seven layers of ashes in a vertical line.

The customary fuel was hazelwood, but evidence of Scots pine and ash tree were found. At

White Park Bay towards Port Braddan.   Oil 24" x 36"

the fourth level charred grain was spread over an extensive floor area, probably barley, rye and wheat. Grain requires milling, so were looked for a quern. There was great excitement the day we found part of a rotary hand mill near the entrance and within seven feet of the roof.

Numerous animal and fish bones were discovered, many split for marrow extraction. Some showed signs of gnawing, although we found no canine bones! Shells and bones indicate the daily menu of the Port Braddan cave dwellers. Ox was the favourite meat – it came from a breed of small cattle similar to those of the Roman period in Britain.[5] Venison, horsemeat, mutton, bacon, fowl, codfish, rudd, limpets, winkles, mussels, whelks and scallops, all featured on the diet sheet of these primitive people.

At least three of our female ancestors left their bones in the cave. A right handed girl of sixteen was found on what we called the third level. At the fourth, the remains of two women revisited our story. One was an adult, probably related to the teenager. The other a twenty year old woman. The later had a narrow nose and a long head, she liked to sit with her knees drawn up and her heels close to each other. This young lady was not related to the other females.

In their early development days, the cave dwellers discovered the superiority of bone over wood for tool manufactory. Some artifices show skill, ingenuity and excellent workmanship. We found piercers and awls made from limb bones or stags' antlers, also a knife blade carved from a rib bone. Three needles produced from the jaw bones of codfish amazed us with their perfection. Eight ivory dress pins, equally perfect, came to light, probably carved from walrus tusks.

At the fifth level we discovered a broken comb. Thirty-nine of the original ninety six teeth were intact, showing the skilful beauty of this early fashion aid. Two ranks of teeth were fashioned on both sides of the comb. Its seven separate plates were held together by two decorated bone binders, these were clamped by five iron rivets. It is impossible to appreciate the time and expertise required to manufacture such a little gem.

Our most beautiful find was a hollow cone-shaped cruet of bone. It is sixty millimetres in length, ending in a point. The rim is a single millimetre in thickness and the diameter only thirteen millimetres!

A highly polished ball stopper with a conical point, fitted snugly into the tiny mouth of the cone-shaped cruet. When we removed the stopper, we found the receptacle had been filled with iron ore. When one thinks how often little objects are lost today, it is amazing that this beautiful item was waiting to be found after thousands of years. That its tiny ball stopper was still in place, is something of a miracle.

At level six we found a rude stone figurine. It represented a human head and torso fashioned from a basalt stone, twelve by five inches in size. The "idol" was leaning against another stone on the east side of the cave. A similar small clay figurine of a fertility goddess was found in a neighbouring cave.

A charming miniature vessel, hollowed from a chalk nodule, was unearthed at level three. It is only twelve millimetres in height and thirty-two in diameter. Its cavity is seven millimetres in depth and twelve in width. Perhaps, it was a toy or a crucible for mixing paint or dye. The comb, shell castles on the beach, the finely manufactured cruet and the beautiful little crucible, personalised the Port Braddan cave for me and made the excavation more than a worthwhile experience.

A profusion of pottery sherds became available for our studies, mostly well fired and similar to those found in the Ballintoy caves. We collected one group of coarse specimens; our second group consisted of sherds from decorated globular pots with finely curving necks and elegantly rounded shoulders.

Most of the sherds were black in colour, occasionally the surface was red, brown or grey.

Some were at the biscuit state[6] although others appear to have been varnished. Decoration was simple - double rows of clean cut finger nail marks, lines drawn with shells, rings of puncture marks, lattice work incisions and delicate fingertip rim indentations. The only sherd which showed marks of wheel-turning belonged to the mediaeval period and was coated with transparent glaze. We found it under the cobbled floor at level eight.

Research on pottery sherds was extremely painstaking but very rewarding. While the study was in progress we examined seventy-two flakes and cores of flints. They were scattered through several levels, we sorted them into four groups. The study of flints is more satisfactory than sherds as the researcher has in hand the actual article in its entirety, not merely a broken piece from it.

There is no evidence of manufacture of items within the cave itself. Perhaps the Port Braddan artisans laboured in the flint factory at White Park Bay and did not take their work home after a long day at the cliff face! The vast number of flint chips on Portacallan bay may indicate they preferred a sunshine and riverside work place to their shadowed cave.

The first group of flints consists of heavy core hand axes, a coarse leaf flake, a borer and several scrapers. The colour ranged through brown, cream and grey; most were water rolled and better fabricated than the later dated second group.

Into the second group we placed a thick knife flake, chipped along the edge for finger rest. Also there is a scraper, thinned all round to a knife-edge, still efficiently serviceable.

All flints in the third groups appear to have been struck from the same creamy-brown nodules. A triangular flake had been worked into a point, apparently to make an engraving tool. A thick flake had been reworked from an earlier tool, in order to make a gouge. A thin leaf flake was cut to make a borer, and a round flake trimmed to form a scraper.

Our fourth group contained a flake with a squared point, a much used triangular borer and a fish tail scraper.

We were equally fascinated with the collection of stone tools, fashioned from basalt, granite, sandstone, quartzite and schist. We found hammers, anvils, rubbers, polishers, hones, sharpeners and even a few combination tools.

Of the several hammers, the most interesting was manufactured from water rolled basalt. It is oval in shape with a pointed end and convenient grooves for finger control. Several anvils came to light – usually made from well chosen flattish and triangular seashore stones. The best hone was made from local red sandstone and shows usage on both sides. It seems our ancestors found basalt inferior to sandstone when it came to making stones to sharpen various implements.

In my letter to your mill I have written a summary of the items we excavated from your local cave in the months before the second world war commenced in 1939. I have given you a short insight of the lifestyle of the early residents of Port Braddan. Your first neighbours were not the only cave dwellers in North Antrim. Similar evidence has come to light in the Park cave at Ballintoy, at Larrybane, Aghalee, Doonmore, Kilbride and on the sandhills at the mouth of the River Bann. Of course, you will know only too well that the splendid view from your mill overlooks White Park Bay where bronze age people built the Tumulus and *"early man went to the seaside"* but that, as they say, is a letter for another day".[7]

"Exegerunt Monuimentum Aere Perennius"[8]

AUTHORS NOTES

1. Portacallan – the noisy inlet.
2. Bones found in caves, and middens indicate domesticated wolves were being used as hunting and guard dogs from the New Stone Age onwards. Dogs were the faithful friends of Australian and American aborigines long before European settlers arrived.
3. Molluscs are invertebrates with soft unsegmented bodies, usually aquatic and protected by shells. (Clams, snails, slugs, squid, and octopus) from Latin Molluscus meaning *A "Thin-Shelled Nut"*.
4. The huge Victorian kitchen range of yesterday and the present day *"Aga"* cooker offer similar facilities by similar methods!
5. The earliest domesticated type of cattle (Bos) was the Celtic or marsh ox of the Stone Age. It was small, short horned with fine limbs and a long forehead. From Latin *"Capitale"* meaning *"Funds"*.
6. 'Biscuit State' – unglazed pottery which has been fired but not glazed. *"Biscuit Firing"* is the first firing at a low temperature. From old French *'Bescuit'* meaning *'Twice-Cooked,* via Latin *'bis'* twice plus *'coquere'* to cook.
7. Most of the Port Braddan collection is in the keeping of the Ulster Museum at Stranmillis, Belfast. Andrew McLean May died on December 13, 1971, in his 92nd year. He was in charge of the Tropical House of the Edinburgh Royal Botanic Gardens before work in N.I. with the Ministry of Agriculture. His research included archaeological sites on the lower Bann, Portstewart and Garvagh.
8. *"They set up a monument more lasting than brass"* (from Horace).

II THE SAINT'S LETTER

Gobban.   Port Braddan c.650

Now that I am staring my Red Letter Valete Day in the face, I really think the best times of my life were those spent beside the port of the salmon on that splendid north coast of Erin's Island. Today I am in France, tied hand and foot by a band of pagan brigands who may well take my life - for I have nought else to give them. So I am recalling all the cheerful days, before I go happily to meet my Maker.

My name is Gobban sometimes Gobhan or Gobain, as they call me here in the uncouth land of the Franks. I was born in the early years of the seventh Christian century in the Kingdom of Ulaid, within the region we call Dal Fiatach on the shores of Lough Lao.[1] Our family lives at Ard-Mac-Nasca. It was a grand place for a boys' playground. Lough Lao was on one side, Lough Cuan lay on the other.[2] There were forests, rivers, low hills and high hills all sitting down together. The great abbey of Bangor was a few miles to the east and to the south lay the monasteries of Movilla and Nendrum.[3]

With my siblings, Laiseran and Graphan we commenced our early education in Bangor. As sons of the leading family we were destined for the ecclesiastical profession. So when the time came we joined a group of twelve young monks to serve our apprenticeship at Inis Pic Monastery - possibly the best school in Ireland, at that time.

Life at Innis Pic was severe but rewarding - fashioning us for the hard life in the Christian clergy. We lived in huts constructed from sally and dab, and thatched with reeds. Each hut accommodated six monks - three old men and three young men. We looked after the vegetable gardens which surrounded our dwellings. We were taught to fish, to mill, to scribe and to sing; generally we learned to do everything for self-support and to live a life of devotion.

Worship in song, prayer and meditation controlled our lives; the monastery bell keeping us on time. Each hut group was organised to perform the worship office in rotation, so that praise on Innis Pic went on continuously day and night.

There was an assembly chapel for Mass. On the campus there was a school, a hospital, a guest house, a mill and a stout palisade - as much to keep trainees inside, as to keep others outside!

My coz and gossip, Laiseran, returned home when we graduated from school to become deacons. He established the Priory at Ard-Mac-Nasca, under the supervision of our old school at Bangor.

Unlike myself, Laiseran became rather famous as his name appeared on a letter to the Holy Father in 642. Some of his intellectual friends were making an inquiry to headquarters regarding the correct method of calculating the date of Easter.[4] Laiseran always was the clever clogs of the family. I am better at using my hands with building materials.[5]

Perhaps it was my architectural skills which prompted my bishop to send me up the great northern road from Tara to Dunseverick, the highway which connected Ireland with the country we now call Scotland across the sea of Moyle.

Dunseverick was my first parish. The castle was one of Ulster's leading houses. It is situated in the

Templastragh Farm. Watercolour 14" x 10". – D. McPherson

sub division of Dal Riata - the tribe of Reuda. It is about sixty miles from our home at Ard-Mac-Nasca.

When I arrived, Dunseverick already had a thousand years of history to its credit. Saint Patrick himself had visited the Dun and blessed the little well at the foot of the cliff. It became a holy well and was of great service to the local folk. Many people will tell you he also blessed the miracle well which clings on the cliff edge, yet never runs dry of water.

Some folk say Saint Patrick consecrated Olcan to be Bishop of Arhimuy in our church at Templastragh. I do not see how this could have happened unless Conal Cearnac of Dunseverick, Red Branch Knight, built Templastragh when he returned after Our Lord's crucifixion. I think Olcan was a missionary priest to our area and was set aside for his work at Dunseverick Castle itself. Later Templastragh became the castle church.

My ministry on the Cloughananavowry Coast - that is the causeway of the Formorians - was exceptionally successful. The people were friendly and most willing to accept the good news of the Christian gospel.

As a result, God sent angelic messengers to discover the special gift I craved as a reward for my missionary efforts and good works. I replied that I lacked nothing. The magnificence of White Park Bay and the grandeur of the Causeway were reward enough for me!

Each time the angels arrived, I sent them away. As this happened on twenty-nine occasions, I became much confused by the frequent angelic visitations and decided to request some impossible reward. I asked for the gift of being able to do good without knowing that I was doing it. I thought this would dissuade the holy messengers.

Of course, all things are possible to God. He decreed that when the sun shines on my face so that my shadow falls behind me, whomsoever my shadow touches will be blessed. Just like Saint Peter in the Acts of the Apostles.

I was very pleased to receive this special talent. As a thanksgiving offering, I decided to build a new church to the glory of God, who gave me ability to bless my flock in so many ways.

I determined to build my church near the sea, between Dunseverick and the White Park. However, each time I built by day, those same angels came in the night to throw it down! Thus they sought to repay me for all the trouble I had given them.

Every time the angels demolished my architectural efforts they put a light on a place where I should try another foundation. This happened on twenty-nine occasions, until the vengeful angels thought I had been punished sufficiently.

On my thirtieth attempt the angels allowed my church to stand. In the year of our blessed Lord, 646, my bishop dedicated it to Saint Lassara. It is called Templastragh, *"the church of the flames"*. It has become the chapel of ease to the castle. The little town, which is growing up quickly on the highway at the top of the lane leading to the church, is called Templastragh.

After my work at Dunseverick was completed I went with my good friend, Saint Fursey, to East Anglia. Clergy were rather thin on the ground in those days, only Erin had a surplus of priests. From my school at Bangor on the Lough of the Calf in Dal Fiatch, missionaries went all over the continent establishing Christian churches.[6]

In East Anglia, King Sigebert donated land near

Saint Gobbans proprietary Chapel.

Yarmouth where we built the monastery of Burglin. It conformed to the Celtic order.

As I have told you building and architecture is my talent, hobby and joy. Of writing I have but little skill. When my work at Burglin was finished, I joined Saint Ultan on the mission to Gaul. This was shortly after the coalition of Germanic, Frankish and other nations which had conquered Gaul. Everything was in turbulence. Our vocation for peace in our time was most necessary. On that pilgrimage we built the monastery at Fosses.

Now I am old and tired. With my bishop's permission , I have decided to become a solitary in the beautiful forest area beside the river Oise. I am building another little community here at Premontre. The valley is very similar to the dear remembered green shores of Lough Laoigh. This evening, as I write, it is mid-summer and the golden light reminds me much of my Irish home. As I have told you a band of brigands holds me here threatening my death.

Give the blessing of my shadow to the people at Ard-Mac-Nasca and Templastragh. I shall see them again only in heaven.

"Amor Omnia Vincit Ad Majorem Dei Gloriam.[7]"

Author's Comments:

St Gobban did not survive the attentions of "The Band of Brigands". He was murdered on 2nd June, which date is his Red Letter Day. The place became known as St Gobain on the River Oise in France.

The foundation date for the original church at Templastragh is suggested as AD648, (G.A. Birmingham and Rev. George Hill).

The celtic folk story of church demolition and rebuilding, where a mysterious light appears, is found in many Irish parishes.

The number twenty nine is an obvious and usual Irish exaggeration. "Many" would be a better choice. There is evidence of several sites in the townland.

Early buildings were constructed of sally and dab - easily burnt or thrown down. After the Norman Conquest (1177) elaborate masonry buildings were constructed. The present Templastragh ruin (early 16th century) appeared to have been a chapel of

East Window St. Gobban's Church

ease and keel for Billy parish and was connected with Dunseverick castle. The local congregation may have transferred to Ballintoy church when it became a parish separated from Billy. O'Laverty claims a freestone altar was still in situ at the east end of the building in 1780.

Ordnance Survey Memoirs (1838) suggest the church was destroyed by Cromwell. The Memoirs record that Cooper Daniel Lamon removed stones from the altar. As a result he took the bloody flux and in 1813 was killed when he fell over a bridge near Ballintoy!

The celtic cross presently built into the west gable was found in a ditch beside a field named Carnabahn - the white carn. No trace of a carn remains, although the whole countryside is covered with antiquities! G.A. Birmingham suggests the stone may date back to the original building. In 1962 the author acquired property at Portbraddan below the present day Templastragh ruin. The Celtic folk story concerning several destroyed ecclesiastical sites in the small townland of Templastragh inspired restoration of what may have been the foundations of one of the churches, as a proprietary chapel. Previously the little building had been used by John McKay as a calf house. Thus the charitable works of St Gobban continue into the twenty first century.[8]

AUTHOR'S NOTES

1. Ulaidh - original tribal meaning is obscure. Generally means Ulstermen, when Tir (Land) is added it gives Ulster. First used in Norse times; first recorded by the Normans. Dal Fiatch was the present County Down; Dal Riata was North Antrim. Lough Lao was the name for Belfast Lough. Lao means a calf and refers to the bovine goddess who lived in the river Lagan, or river Lao. The later Lagan means Low Lying.

2. Ard-Mac-Nasca - Height of the son of Nasca. (See 'Holywood Then and Now'). Local chief Nasca is buried in the Cairn Hill behind the town. His son was Laiseran, who built the first Christian settlement in Holywood (Sanctus Boscus). Lough Cuan was Strangford Lough - Cuan means Sea-inlet of bays. The later 'Stranger' means 'strong' or violent (sea-inlet).

3. Bangor Abbey - Banagher means 'pointed', possibly the points of land at the entrance to Bangor Bay. Here St. Comgall founded a monastery c.558. Movilla - 'plain of the sacred tree' at Newtownards, where St. Finian founded a monastery c. 540. Nendrum - 'single ridge'. St. Mochaoi founded a monastery on Island Mahee, Strangford Lough in the fifth century.

4. Bede lists Laiseran among the Irish clergy who obtained instruction from Rome in 642 regarding the correct method of calculating the annual date of Easter (see Ecclesiastical History of the English Nation (735)).

5. St. Gobban was thought to be a craftsman, church builder, or architect. His name appears in other places in Co. Antrim and Co. Down, also in England and France.

6. Missionaries from Bangor went to Gaul, Switzerland, Germany, Austria and Italy. Moluag became prominent in Scotland and Columbanus in Bobbio. Early collections of annals were written in Bangor and an 'exotic' Latin was developed in the Bangor Antiphony (see Adamsons: 'Bangor Light of the World').

7. "Love conquers everything to the greater glory of God."

8. Each time donations from visitors and wedding guests come to one thousand pounds, a new charity benefits from their generosity. Thus Saint Gobban's shadow of blessing continues into the twenty first Christian century. Your donation is included in the purchase price of this book. The following charities wish to thank St. Gobban.

1.	National Trust	8.	M S Society
2.	Corrymeela Community	9.	Omagh Memorial Trust
3.	N. I. Hospice	10.	Princess of Wales Trust
4.	N I Children's Hospice	11.	Camphill Community (Glencraig)
5.	Marie Currie Trust	12.	Alzmiers Society
6.	Missions to Seamen	13.	U.S.P.C.A. (Coleraine)
7.	Cystic Fibrosis Society	14.	U.S.P.Countryside
15.	Concern for Africa	16.	McMillan Cancer Trust

17. Fleming Fulton School. Two donations to help provide training facilities for paralympic paraplegics.

18. Guide Dogs for the Blind. Five donations to buy dogs called Gobban, Braddan, Finn, Bush and Moyle.

19. R.N. Lifeboat Institute. Two donations, the second to purchase a survival seat in the new Portrush Lifeboat.

20. Men Against Cancer. Current donations will help to establish a diagnostic unit and research programme at the Belfast City Hospital for treatment of all types of cancer among men.

21 The first donation was to the Youth Hostel Association. Thousands of backpackers from the White Park Bay Hostel have visited St. Gobban in Port Braddan, he could be called a life member of the Association.

III THE SPANISH CAPTAINS LETTER

CAPTAIN FRANCISCO DE CUELLAR . THE ARMADA 1588

For many months I have sought a way in which to declare my gratitude to your good Irish folk who risked life and limb to save me after the annihilation of La Armada Invincible et Felicissima. So I am right pleased to pen this epistle to your little mill situated on that cold ragged Causeway Coast. Close to Port Braddan is Dunluce Castle where our good Spanish galleass *Girona* of The Naples squadron, perished on Friday, October 18, 1588. I came to Dunluce in great distress and affliction the following year, on January 11. Your good Irish neighbours cared for me in the hills behind White Park Bay until February 21, when your local Catholic bishop procured a safe passage to Scotland for our group of Spanish refugees.

All this I shall record later. First let me tell you the cause of the terrible disaster which fell upon my country by reason of the English Virgin Queen. I am Captain Don Francisco de Cuellar, my ship was San Pedro, a galleon of the twenty-four such good ships which belonged to the Castieles Squadron. I am writing to you from a prison in Antwerp. The date is October 1589. Please allow your countrymen to understand the true story of our ruinous calamity.

Our gracious majesty, Philip II of Spain was utterly exasperated by the scandalous actions of the English Queen. Her sea captains had stolen millions of gold ducats from our Spanish ships, our Ambassador had been expelled, the English people were fast becoming heretics, and that dragon Drake was boasting that he had singed his Majesty's beard. The last straw, which broke the Spanish camel's back, was the bloody execution of Mary, Queen of Scots, in February 1587.

Our invasion fleet sailed out of Lisbon in May 1588. I was proud to be captain of my spanking *San Pedro*, my men cheered loudly as we crossed the harbour bar. Under sail were 65 warships, 25 transports, 4 galleys, 4 galleasses and more than 32 small vessels. Among the last were many fast dispatch boats, because the King required daily reports of our movements. We had 19,295 soldiers and 8050 sailors, besides clerics and others. We carried 2431 weapons and great quantities of shot and powder. Our commander in chief was the famous Duke of Medina Sidonia, Order of the Golden Fleece.[1] We were to rendezvous with another invasion force, commanded by the great Duke of Parma, which was to be conveyed in barges from the Low Countries. After that, our sailing orders were to cross the few miles over the Channel and invade England.

No sooner had we parted from Lisbon on a fair wind, than a nor' wester hit us with such great force that the entire fleet was driven southwards. Prayers were offered on all the ships and the wind shifted to a strong south' wester thanks be to God; we were able to pursue our intention of the invasion of England.

We sighted Cape Finisterre and were tacking to starboard off La Corunna when a fierce gale fell upon us. This was most unusual for the month of

Girona   (from the Effingham tapestries).

May. The fleet dispersed and many ships rendered the worse for wear and tear.

I know you are a sailing man yourself. Have you ever had to tack, beating to windward in the middle of a fleet of 129 other vessels of all sizes, speeds and sailing ability? Is it any wonder so many of our ships were damaged, including my own San Pedro.

It took us nineteen days to make Corunna. Here we hoped to meet with victuallers to amend ships' stores, some of which had been destroyed in the storm, most of which had been supplied, already rotten, by fraudulent Spanish contractors. We required fresh water even more than provisions, as our barrels had been made of unseasoned wood and the water therein was stinking green. Drinking whereof caused gastric fevers. We tossed around for a full week and no provision ships appeared, although the Captain General sent urgent letters to the King everyday.

Another storm was approaching, so the Duke himself with 38 ships of the line, of which I was one, decided to go into La Corunna to make arrangements for taking up provisions and setting down the sick.

A most violent storm broke upon us that very night. At first light the horizon was empty of our ships, which had been cruising in wait for the Captain General to return and give the signal to proceed.

Here then was a pickle. It appeared our leader had deserted his post informing only 38 ships of his intentions! *"Death for any who forsook the Captain General's wake to shelter in a Spanish port"*. I was safe which ever way the law decided – would that I had known what was in store!

The Duke was mightily relieved when messages started to arrive – *"10 damaged ships be at Vivero; 2 galleases are in bad shape at Gijon, the Girona is in need of repairs to tillers, rigging and prow."* A search was fitted out for the missing Armada. Before we had set out on May 20th, Kings orders were to rendezvous at the Scilly Islands, should the fleet be scattered for any reason. That was good thinking on behalf of our leaders. Now a couple of very fast oared patches were dispatched to discover if any of the missing ships had gained the Scilly Isles. However, two galleases and 21 other ships were unaccounted, that is an accommodation of 8,500 men!

Imagine our situation. December weather in June, vomiting crews unable to eat and nothing to eat anyway. Only green slimy water to drink. The fleet split up, many ships damaged, no replacements available, inexperienced crews and over optimistic commanders on shore. All this even before we had met the enemy!

On June 24 the Duke, most audaciously, advised the King to seek an honourable agreement with the English before it was too late. The Duke of Parma was equally defeatist. *"My men are cold, wet, sick and hungry. The death roll increases every week"*.

His Majesty replied by return on June 26 and July 1st. *"My intention is clear to you, which is not to withdraw but to complete what has been started, overcoming all obstacles. Send a daily courier. Get under sail the day you receive My order."* Then on the 30th we were told all the ships had been located and repairs were in operation. As for the sick, the Archbishop of Santiago had established a miracle working hospital for all comers! We doubted all this, but dared not say a contrary word.

The promised order came from His Majesty on July 12. *"Start the voyage the day you receive this* letter, even if you leave some ships behind". So the father confessors assembled on an island in the harbour and every one of us received the Blessed Sacrament. We prayed for a safe voyage and a favourable wind.

During the night of July 23rd God sent the propitious breeze, we heard the signal from the Duke's ships and off we sailed, but for two hours only! Then came a second cannon roar. *Zuniga's* rudder hinges had come asunder; we had another day of boredom waiting for her steering equipment to be repaired.[2]

Now the waiting time was over and we were making sail for the defence of Spain and the invasion of England, a voyage of only a few nautical miles. When I returned a year later, I saw the volumes of misleading information, propaganda, rumours and deliberate falsehood with which the people at home had been fed. So I shall set down what actually happened during that *"Annus armorum nauticorum"*.

As I say, we sailed on July 23rd, on the afternoon of Friday 29th at four of the clock or eight bells as we say, we heard the three cannon shots signal *"For every man to offer prayer before battle."* As it got dark we saw the English beacons blazing war fires from headland to headland; for we were off the Lizard and in our usual crescent formation.

The English admiral, Francis Drake, *"El Draque"* as we called him, had sixty ships ready at Plymouth on the ebb tide. At moonrise our look-outs saw white shadows sailing on the horizon. First light, the following morning, revealed eighty ships astern of our fleet to seaward and windward. We were in our ordered crescent formation with our best ships placed in the foremost positions. We longed for the English to close with us, so that we could engage them in battle.

However, we could only gaze in admiration at the incredible speed and expert manoeuvrability of eleven of these little English ships. With rapid tack on track, they beat up within a whisker of the wind. Seemingly without effort they joined the other English ships, which had swept around our Armada under cover of darkness.

My God, but they were like little devils, a shoal of silver flying fish, to our clumsy black whales! We knew the calm blue Mediterranean waters and winds. They knew this turbulent channel with its unpredictable currents and hurricanes. Our ships were castles floating on the sea, huge rowing boats with sails. Our standing orders were to close in, board the enemy and let our soldiers take the hostile ship. The English relied on accurate marksmanship combined with efficient navigation and velocity.[3] We presented large slow targets to these little speed boats; they struck and left us in their wakes. All their ships were fighters. Of our fleet of 130 ships, only fifty were men of war.

My crew and I saw from *San Pedro* that we had no chance of success. The English were chivvying us up the Channel like a little pack of terriers after a large pack of rats! And then there was that infernal wind, as their infidel Queen inscribed on her accursed medals *"Afflavit Deus"* – *"God blew with his wind and they were scattered".*

We could do none other than slouch up the Channel, the English easily picking off those who fell too far behind. We tried to engage the enemy on three occasions – once in the open sea, then off St. Alban's Head and St. Catherines Point, losing confidence all the way. On August 6th the Duke ordered Armada to anchor at Calais.

The English had revictualled from the Cinque Ports, and taken on additional sailors. We desperately required provisions, water and shot.

Antrim Headlands and Dunluce. Oil 20" x 20".

Then shortly after midnight wild cries spread from ship to ship, *"FIRE FIRE FIRE"*. A line of blazing vessels, borne on wind and gales, was closing on us rapidly. We thought this wall of fire was the Hellburners of Antwerp, by which secret weapon we had been tricked some three years previously.[4] We recalled the fatal accident of only a week before, when San Salvador, exploded like a fascinating fireworks display, reflected on the water[5]. Fighting to the death or drowning are to be expected by sailors; to be burnt alive is something else entirely!

All hell broke loose. Orders resounded to cut the cables and hoist the sails, ships rammed neighbours, others drifted into the current or got caught up in the rigging. Confusion, collision and contention raged on every side. At dawn, on August 8th we realised that the great Spanish fleet was scattered from Calais to Gravelines. The English saw their opportunity and lost no time in efficient naval attack. Our ships were picked off one by one, as chance offered, before we could reform in any sort of order.

We licked our wounds during the pitch black night of August 7 to 8. Anchors were lost, rudders fouled, gudgeons destroyed, sails in tatters and worst of all, our confidence in the world's greater Armada, completely evaporated! We were a sorry shadow of the unsinkable fleet which had proudly sailed from Lisbon, nine weeks previously.

Now occurred an incident which almost ended my naval career before it had properly started. As I have told you my ship, *San Pedro,* had sustained great damage, as had many others. Things being quiet, I went below to my cabin to rest, for I had not seen the inside of my hammock for ten days. While I slept, the mate sailed a couple of miles ahead of the Admiral's ship in order to effect the necessary repairs in preparation for departure. Hardly had I risen from my pit, than a tender from the Admiral came alongside with orders for me to report immediately. I though I was to receive some well-deserved commendation, so I made haste to comply with the order. How wrong one can be! I was charged with proceeding the Admiral's ship in the line and condemned to death in the most ignominious manner. I was angry and astonished. As a Spanish captain I appealed to the Judge Advocate who was with the fleet, Martin de Aranda, a great gentleman.

I was taken to his ship. The Judge Advocate listened most courteously to my case, he exonerated me completely and kept me with his own entourage. I had lost command of my own ship but I had kept my head on my shoulders. I knelt on the deck and thanked Blessed Mother Mary. As things turned out, as you will shortly read, had I returned to *"San Pedro"* I should have been lost with the rest of my crew.

However, my friend Don Cristobal de Auila, the captain of a store ship, who also had transgressed by proceeding the Admiral, received no mercy. He was hanged from the yardarm with great cruelty and ignominy, even though he was a high born Spanish gentleman like myself.

Our great fleet plundered onward pursued by the English vessels. And now another hazard trap threatened some of our ships. A great swell was rushing and the wind was in the north west. The crippled Spanish ships were being driven unto the Zeeland Banks! *"Better drowned than burned; better sunk than captured"*. We made our confessions, celebrated the Eucharist and made our peace with God and Man. Then came a miracle – I can call it nothing else. At the last minute the wind changed to the south west, the sails filled and we sallied to safety on the noon day bell. Regretfully we had to leave San Mateo and San Felipe to their fate, two of our best ships of the line.

The following day, August 10, 1588, a warm south wester was carrying us up the channel at a spanking speed. We passed the dreaded Dogger Bank to port with the English sheep dogs following all the way. By the time we passed the Firth of Forth, without any sign of attempting a landing, they realised we were in full fight and intended to return to Spain by the northern route. Drake sailed home in triumph leaving a couple of ships to keep us in sight in case we changed our minds!

Four hundred miles of open Atlantic ocean lay before us. We got into some sort of formation – 95 ships manned by thousands of sick sailors. The Admiral issued orders to return to Spain on a carefully specified course, with a warning to avoid the savages of Hibernia.

Daily rations were cut down to half a pound of salt biscuits, a pint of water and half a pint of wine. Would that we had possessed such provisions – our pints of water had to be collected from the sky! Those ships which carried horses and mules were ordered to toss them over board to save fresh water.

Some ships deserted. On August 15 we captured three Scottish fishing boats, the sailors of which were forced to serve us as pilots for the voyage around the Orkney and Shetland Islands.

It was then that freezing fog descended. Eerie, silent and skinning days followed, in seas we did not know, mostly lying motionless. By the 18th we had cleared the Orkneys and by September 3rd the Hebrides were astern.

San Martin claimed to be the first ship to get back to Spain safely, 1500 miles in fifteen days! It took several weeks for sixty-five surviving vessels to gain Spanish ports, bringing typhoid, bronchitis, dysentery and death in their holds. All this I heard over a year later, for I was with the other half of the Armada ships which never returned to Spain.

On September 20, 1588 I was shipwrecked on the Streedagh shore of Sligo Bay in western Ireland.[6] By God's good grace we had avoided Tory island and passed it to port. But our pumps could not empty the bilge. Our spars were damaged and our sails gone.

Three of our ships had stayed in sight of each other as we rounded the north-west corner of Ireland. When the horrific Atlantic gales hit us our cables parted and we were driven into Sligo Bay for safety. We anchored a mile off shore to make the necessary repairs for a homeward voyage, after the storms had subsided.

Here we remained for four long days, working on the ships and recovering our strength. Then on the fifth day such a great storm hurled itself upon our beam, that we were driven unto the beach. With great difficulty we avoided the jagged rock cliffs which framed the sand, but within the hour the ships were completely destroyed by the surf. More than a thousand men were drowned. Three hundred came to shore alive, mostly captains, officials and other persons of rank.

All this I observed from the poop deck of the Judge Advocate's ship. From this vantage point I witnessed the awful spectacle of many sailors drowning in their ships, because they would not jump overboard; others having cast themselves into the surf were sucked below never to return to the surface. A few on rafts, barrels and pieces of ship got to shore safe and sound.

However, when they reached the shore alive

many were butchered by English soldiers and Irish natives for the Spanish clothing and treasures they possessed. Don Diego Enriquez, captain of San Juan ordered out his decked longboat and accompanied by Count Villa Franca and other gentlemen, locked themselves into the hold with 16,000 ducats. The crew pushed this life-boat overboard and seventy of them jumped unto the deck and to their deaths. The longboat got to shore upside-down! Its passengers were suffocated, except for Don Diego. The next day the Irish natives broke open the cabin, removed all the treasures and left the Count to die.

My landfall was more propitious. I remained on the ship and left it at the last possible moment with the aid of our Lady of Contanar. Then, clinging to a huge circular hatch gate, I rolled overboard. Its weight submerged me for so long a time that I thought it impossible to live without fresh air. At last I surfaced and drew Martin de Aranda unto my raft. He had saved my life, now I attempted to return the compliment. *My God* he was heavy! He had a treasury of gold pieces stitched into his waist coat and trousers. A wave washed him off the hatch gate, which then overturned and crushed my legs.

The Blessed Virgin sent four waves to carry me to shore, so bleeding and broken that the soldiers and Irish natives thought me already dead. In this sorry condition I hobbled along the sand and soon met with a young Spanish gentleman quite concussed from the wreck.

Twilight approached, it was my first night on Irish soil. As you will know very well, it does not get really dark at that time of the year in your country. Dusk and dawn are almost one, and if there be a moon there is little night, such as we have in Spain.

Two Irishmen approached us, one carried a battleaxe the other a pistol. They shouted at us, but we feigned ignorance, which required little acting ability. They hacked down a bed of rushes for us and signalled us to lie down. Then they covered us with dry grass and bid us a good night. In soothe, this was a kind action! Later I discovered that the Irish treat idiots with great respect as God's gift to their communities.

After the natives had parted from us they went on to the beach to use the battle axe on the money chests which had come to shore from our ships. Under the dry grass my companion and I fell into the sleep of the just.

About one of the clock, I was roused by a troop of English horsemen going to plunder our ships. I tried to rouse my friend in case we should be discovered. I found that the youth had died in his sleep. I had to leave him there with thousands of my fellow Spaniards – to be devoured by black crows, brown rats and wild dogs.

There was no point in returning to my bed of reeds and grass so I walked along Streedagh shore to find any Spaniards whom I could assist. For nigh on three miles the sand was strewn with great timbers of wrecked vessels, the vast amount would have built many ships. There were cables , cordage, masts, spars and all the flotsam and jetsam which would have furnished many mansions.

I extracted whatever clothing I could find in the debris and some little food. Then I went into hiding for the remainder of the day, as the Irish natives were crowding the beach looking for salvage. From my refuge I witnessed many deathly blows as the natives fought over fine pieces of carved Spanish mahogany and other treasures.

At dawn I determined to get away from this

terrible place. Perhaps I could find a monastery or convent where I could claim sanctuary. After much effort, for my legs and feet were very weak and sore, I came upon a church and entered joyfully, thanking Saint Christopher for his guidance.

The place was deserted, the images of the holy saints were chared with fire. Seven corpses of my Spanish comrades were swinging from the window bars. The English heretical soldiers had desecrated the holy place. As with other shrines in the area, they had made them into pigsties and cow byres, sending the Catholic clergy packing.

This taught me a salutary lesson. I must keep hidden from the English soldiers, for they were going up and down the country dispatching the Spaniards, who had escaped from the perils of the sea.

Afterward I discovered the church was dedicated to St Molaise and the deserted monastery was called Staad Abbey[7]. I knelt and prayed at the ruined altar, begging my blessed Lady for safe return to Spain.

The lane from the abbey lay through a great forest which stretched behind the sea-shore. Herein I wandered seeking food, blackberries and nuts. When I limped along for about a mile, I met an old hag. She was driving her cows into the forest, to hide them from the English soldiers, who had been billeted in her village. By signs she indicated her sorrow for my afflictions and would have had me at her cottage but that the English would cut my throat. She warned me to go no further along the path.

I thought it best to return to the shore where I knew I could find provisions. Here I was joined by two Spaniards, one wounded in the head the other pitifully mangled. In our search for food, we found more than salt washed biscuits on the sands! Four hundred Spanish corpses lay together near the place where their ship was broken. To my horror, I espied two friends and took time to bury the corpses in the sand, offer a requiescat and mark the grave with a driftwood cross.

At that moment our actions drew the attention of the booty collectors. However, they saw the sign of the Holy Cross on the grave and left us to grieve in peace. When four youths teased us, an old man chastised them, rescued us and directed us towards his village.

The road was stony under my poor feet, the wounds on my legs were festering and I was freezing with cold from loss of blood. I was unable to keep up with my friends and they went ahead.

When I had shambled on a little way I met an ancient man accompanied by two youths and a beautiful maiden. One boy slashed the sinew of my wounded right leg, ripped my clothes, snatched my gold chain and forty five gold crown pieces which I had stitched into my jacket. He also stole the Holy Relics which had been blessed in Lisbon before we commenced this tragic adventure.

The girl hung the chain and relics around her lovely neck, saying she would keep them as she was a Christian. To me, she was the Blessed Virgin herself, for she made the second boy bring a poultice, specially made from healing herbs, which she put on my wounds. Also she made me take supper – oaten bread with creamy butter and a drink of buttermilk.

That was a feast fit for a king and the finest meal I have ever eaten. Afterwards the boy showed me a road to follow, which avoided the village where many Spaniards had been slaughtered. The road led straightway northwards, towards a horizon of blue hills at six leagues distance. The boy told me this was the territory of a clan which favoured the King of Spain. Some eighty of my countrymen were in hiding there, he said.

I took courage and started a special novena for nine days. I set off for the northern side of the hills to the country of a great Irish chief called Sir Brian O'Rourke.

I struggled along as best I could, thanking St. Christopher at every step that my festering wounds had been salved. As darkness fell I reached a few small cabins where I was offered shelter by an Irishman who could speak Latin. He dressed my wounds and prepared a good supper. About midnight his father and brothers arrived, laiden down with plunder from our ships. They were kind folk and pleased that I had visited the cottage for a night's rest.

In the morning they lent me a guideboy and a horse to carry me over the worst part of the mud encrusted road. Soon the boy espied a posse of English soldiers. *"Save yourself Spaniard"* says he *"These Sassenachs are on duty and will slice you into little pieces"*. Rapidly we concealed ourselves in a hiding place, which the boy obviously knew only too well, from previous experiences with English soldiers.

The posse passed on towards the coast and we proceeded, keeping a keen lookout. Then came upon us a band of Irish Lutherans who wished to cut me down to the ground.[8] The boy swore that I was the sick prisoner of his father and he was taking me to be cured! Even so two of these heretical devils struck me to the ground and stripped me naked, before they departed.

This was the only time I wished for death and prayed God that he would fulfil this petition. The boy wept bitter tears with me. It was he who clothed me with a piece of his own blanket and a quantity of bracken fonds to keep off the arctic winds. I was sad to bid him farewell when he had to return homeward. I shall always thank him for bringing me through the lowest part of my adventure. May God grant that this boy be rewarded in life and in death with the same spirit of mercy which he gave me on that dark day.

On I went towards the land of the friendly O'Rourkes. I came to a beautiful lake, which afterwards I found the Irish call Lough Melvin.[9] A village of thirty cabins cosseted the shore. It appeared to be completely deserted. I sought out the best cottage in which to pass the night and found it was a store for oat sheaves. The dry stalks rustled. Terrified, I jumped back from the door. There before me were three naked Spaniards rubbing the sleep from their eyes! Then all was great excitement when they discovered I was their comrade, Captain Cuellar. They nigh killed me with their embraces, for they thought I had been drowned when our ship was wrecked on Streedagh beach.

We buried ourselves in the sheaves for heat and slept soundly until the morning. Fortunately the great pain in my legs awakened me early. Suddenly I heard the cottage door opening and through the sheaves I saw an Irishman with a halberd in his hand. He examined the oats, seemed satisfied and left the cottage. Soon we heard the sound of the farmers reaping and hoeing and singing their sad songs, in the gardens around the village. We dared not show ourselves, for we determined they were Lutherans from their plaintive psalm singing.

When darkness fell, wrapped in straw and hay, we sallied forth by moonlight slithering through the mud and faint with hunger. And so we came to the territory of the O'Rourkes. Although the chief and his warriors were abroad, harrying their English overlords, we found many Spanish refugees assembled for safety in this place.[10]

I was well received in a cottage where the family was extremely kind. They dressed my wounds, gave me food and an Irish blanket to keep out the bitter cold. While we were in this village, news came that a large Spanish ship had arrived at Sligo bay to take off any survivors who could assemble with great speed. Our party of twenty hopefuls hastened towards the coast. The injuries to my legs prevented speed so I missed the sailing by more than a day, thanks be to Our Lady. Everyone of my companions and some two hundred more were drowned or murdered when the ship was wrecked on the accursed Irish coast, a few days later.

As I made my solitary return journey, I fell in with an Irish priest who showed me much Christian charity. We conversed in the Latin tongue and he directed me to Rossclogher castle at some six leagues distance.[11] He said I should receive sanctuary there with the clan MacClancy, who were sub chiefs to the great Irish O'Rourkes.

This good priest produced dinner from his sacellus and shared wine and vitals with me, after he had blessed us in the name of all the Holy Blessed and Indivisible Trinity. Then my journey took me through the beautiful valley of Glenade. Even my injuries and melancholia could not render me immune to the extreme beauty of the rugged Irish countryside – I have seen nothing to equal it in Spain.

Alas, such thoughts were short lived. When my legs and feet were giving me great pain, I fell in with an Irish blacksmith. He offered me food and

Dunluce. Woodcut, 14 x 20 cms. Donald McPherson.

shelter if I would operate the bellows for his forge. He said he would teach me his trade and I should stay there for the rest of my life! I feigned a favourable countenance to him, and to the accursed old hag he had for a wife.

Fortunately the Blessed Virgin sent my friend the Latin-speaking priest to the forge, after eight days of my misery. The holy man was extremely angry and the next day requested the MacClancy to send four servants and a refugee Spanish soldier to convey me to Rossclogher castle.

I was kindly received in the MacClancy family court and there found ten Spaniards who had escaped from shipwrecks. I was clothed in a clean and warm blanket, similar to those worn all over the countryside. During the happy three months which I enjoyed the hospitality of Rossclogher Castle I aimed to please my hosts and became a virtual Irishman like themselves. My friend the priest, who came each week to serve the Mass, laughed at me and said: *"Francisco Hiberniores Hibernicis Ipsis"*[12]

The lady wife of the chief was very beautiful and showed me much kindness. With good food and physical attention my wounds started to heal. One day when we were at play in the castle gardens, enjoying the autumn sunshine, my lady engaged me in conversation. All those of her class can speak the Latin tongue. My lady, surrounded by her beautiful attendants asked me what we did in Spain for entertainment. For jest, I replied we told the fortunes of our Spanish maidens, by reading the lines on their lovely hands. They took to this like sun to summer. The more absurd my stories the better they applauded. I became such a favourite that all my time was spent at the centre of a foolish crowd of maidens and their swains. Everyone wanted to have silly fortunes told.

I had no desire to become a Romany palmist, so the chief kindly gave the order that I should not be troubled with such tomfoolery.

Here I shall tell you something of these kind Irish people – for I had sufficient time to observe their customs during the many days I enjoyed the hospitality of the MacClancy family.

The men are tall, broad, handsome and lithe as roe-deers on the mountains. Their hair is either as black as Spaniards or as red as the setting sun. Their women folk are beautiful in the extreme, slim and seductive with black, auburn or golden tresses. They eat only in the evening, mostly of oaten breads and creamy butter; on feast days they devour badly cooked flesh. Their main drink is buttermilk. They appear to despise water, although the springaqua is the best in the world.

The men wear tight trousers and short loose coats made from goat hair. In cold weather they enwrap in thick woollen blankets. The women folk dress plainly, not having the example of the Spanish court to follow. They wear a chemise under the usual blanket and a linen cloth over their hair.

Both men and women are very great workers and are happy to walk for miles on the slightest provocation. Although they keep the most comfortable beds in their castle and cottages, when necessity requires they will sleep on the bare ground and on rushes, even when recently cut and full of water or ice!

As to religion, the Irish are dedicated to the only true and holy orders of the Catholic Church of Rome. Mass is celebrated wherever possible. However the English heretics and such infidel Irish who have joined them to gain personal advancement from the Queen, have destroyed many monasteries. In short there is neither justice or right in the kingdom, everyone does as he pleases!

As soon as news of the wrecking of our Armada on the far west coast arrived in Dublin, Lord Deputy Fitzwilliam came with 1,700 soldiers to find the ships, kill the escapees and imprison our Irish deliverers.

One Sunday, after Mass, the Mac Clancy himself told us of his decision to take the usual method of protection against the English. With family, treasures and herds, he would retire to the impregnable mountains, till the emergency subsided.

The Mac Clancy informed his Spanish visitors that we should fend for ourselves and look to our own safety. We discussed the situation and determined to ask if we might remain in the fort, and defend it until the Mac Clancy family would return. All of us had sufficient experience of ranging the countryside naked and shivering, dying of hunger and thirst. We had no wish to exchange the comfort of Rossclogher for certain death by the

English army.

We promised to defend the castle to the death or till the family would return from the mountains. The Mac Clancy was pleased and promised to lay in provisions for six months, four boat loads of stones, six muskets, six crossbows and whatever arms he could afford us. This done, the clan left Rossclogher for their retreat in the mountains. We reconnoitred our position: nine gallant Spaniards in a well fortified fort, were more than a match for a company of hungry Sassenachs out in the open.

Let me tell you why we were so confident of success in our venture. The fort is built on an ancient circular mound with foundations of great rocks and earth to above the water-level. The island on which it stands is a hundred yards from the shores of Lough Melvin. The castle entrance has an adequate bastion pierced for musketry. The lake water is very deep and descends sheer from the thick walls. In places Lough Melvin is a league in width and three leagues in length. The surrounding land is a muddy marsh through which only the initiated may travel safely. No army could take this castle without artillery and no artillery could be got within range of it.

So when the English army arrived, it could not get nearer than an Irish mile from the castle walls. The Queen's representative addressed us through a speaking trumpet, with false promises of free passports to Spain when we surrendered. We amused ourselves by shouting *"come closer, we are unable to understand your English"*. He replied by hanging two Spaniards in front of the castle and attempted by all means to instil the fear of God into us.

For seventeen days the English laid futile siege to Rossclogher Castle from Rossfriar point. By then the English soldiers had devoured all the provisions on the mainland and no cover was available for a force of 1,800 men.[14]

Now the wild winter weather fell upon us in all its fury. Severe storms became a daily occurrence. They banked up great snow drifts, many feet in high. The English army were forced to retire and leave us in peace.

Soon the Mac Clancy with his family, stock and treasures returned to his castle. He heaped us with compliments, implored us to become honorary members of his clan and remain in Ireland for ever. To seal this arrangement he offered his sister in marriage with me. In Ireland all such pacts are confirmed in nuptial ties. For this I had no desire, even though the good lady was most beautiful and willing. I had a belly yearning to get home to Spain, that no alchemy could cure. The Mac Clancy, not to be thwarted, declared that *"I should not leave Ireland till the king of Spain himself came to collect me"*.

In the year 1588, a few nights after the Holy Nativity of our Blessed Lord, I slipped away with four friends on a little coracle. As we were acquainted with every secret path through the swamps, we were far away before our absence was discovered.

Later I heard, with great grief, that on April 23, 1590 the head of my friend and deliverer, the Mac Clancy himself, was severed from his body and displayed on the ramparts of the English camp. My other good friend, the O'Rourke was taken to London and hanged for high treason in the same year.

So it was in January 1589, that I commenced the last chapter of my Irish adventure. It took three weeks to make the journey from Lough Melvin in County Donegal to Dunluce Castle in County

Antrim, near to your millhouse. As the proverbial crow files the journey is eighty two miles. On shore by foot, lake and river valley, mountain and desolate plain, it seemed like eight hundred and two miles! Only God knows how I endured the hardships of such a journey!

Dunluce Castle is an ancient erection by the English conquistadors of Ireland.[15] Fortunately, in 1585, the Irish clan MacDonnell had captured the fortress. This clan was most favourable to the Spanish king and had remained within the holy Catholic Church. From Dunluce I knew I should find a passage to Spain.

It was below this great castle that *Girona* our Spanish galleass, had come to grief. She was sister ship to the Naples squadron flagship, *San Lorenzo*. *Girona* reached Sligo Bay some time after we were shipwrecked on Streedagh Shore. Her complement was 551. After major repair she set sail for Scotland from Killybegs, with 1,300 souls crammed unto her decks. On October 16 1588, she foundered on Lacada Point, at the Giants Causeway; only five sailors survived to tell the story.[16]

I reached Dunluce three months after this tragic event and discovered, to my eternal grief, that many of my friends had been lost on the rocks under the castle. I went into the local church to offer many requiescats for the response of their eternal souls.

The people of your countryside offered me much kindness and recounted the great misfortune of our Spanish sailors. They showed me many jewels and treasures which they had salvaged from the wreck of *Girona*. This distressed me greatly.

A family near your mill took me into their cottage. They treated my wounds, because the injuries to my legs and feet had reopened during the long walk from Lough Melvin. The family gave me shelter and food. May the Mother of our Lord bless them for their charity.

It was my chief concern to gain the Scottish shore, which from this part of Ireland is only eleven miles across the North Channel. My cursed leg held me back so that I missed a Scottish bound vessel by two days. But it was of no little happiness to me that the four companions, with whom I had been travelling, got to the quay in time to board that ship.

Again I was alone and in great pain. I was in a country only a few miles from freedom, but a country where English soldiers were as plentiful as blackberries. Again the Blessed Virgin came to my aid and sent me to some women in a village you call Castleroe, which is in the hills behind your mill at Port Braddan.[17]

These good people tended me for the six weeks it took for my poor legs and feet to heal. Then again I set off to find a ship bound for Scotland. Alas, I was taken into custody by two English soldiers, while I was seeking information on the quay. When the young officers started to flirt with a crowd of lively Irish colleens, who saw my difficulty, I took the opportunity to make an escape.

Near to the quay there was a dense thicket of cruel brambles. Into this I hurled myself, preferring the deep scratching of my body to the inside of the local prison! When darkness fell, I sought a safe hiding place. I came upon a lake where two Irish cowherds were bringing in their animals for the evening milking. Again I enjoyed the proverbial Ulster hospitality and stayed for two days recovering from my escapade with the bramble patch.

One of the cowherds went down to the quay to discover how I could make an escape to Scotland. He returned rapidly to report that the two English soldiers were scouring the town for me and had found my cache in the brambles! The boy told me to go to the local bishop who already was giving sanctuary to twelve Spanish sailors. At that very moment, he was making provision for their passage to Scotland. The boy took me to Bishop Redmund O'Gallagher of Derry, who was in the town at that time.

It took six days to make arrangements for the voyage. During that time the good bishop treated me with exceptional kindness and we had many conversations about the politics of our countries.

At dawn a week later, after the celebration of Mass, the bishop provided us with all things necessary for eighteen passengers. So we set sail for Scotland. May God keep this holy bishop and preserve him from his enemies.

We embarked in a wretched little vessel which soon was swamped. The mainsail was carried away in a hurricane, which had sprung up from nowhere. By God's good grace we reached land and waited two days for the wind to abate.[18]

With the arrival of fair weather, we set sail for Scotland once again. It took 3 days to make the short crossing on account of the quantity of saltwater the miserable little boat was shipping.

We had been told that King James VI of Scotland protected all Spaniards who reached his Kingdom. This we soon found to be completely inaccurate. In Scotland I suffered the greatest privations for six months and often wished I was back in Ireland. Had it not been for the Catholic Lords of Scotland, that heretical King would have sold us to his virgin mistress, the Queen of England.

The good Catholic Lords forced their feeble King to commission a Scottish merchant from Flanders to give passage to all Spaniards who had been rescued from the defeated Armada. The merchant provided four ships, at a cost to the Lords of five ducats per head. Also they arranged, at much cost to themselves, safe passports for all English interests.

However, all this was merely treachery, for the true intention of the Scottish merchant was that all of us would be massacred at the entrance to Dunkirk harbour by ships of Holland and Zealand, which would be lying in wait for our arrival.

And there we should have been murdered had not the Blessed Virgin herself intervened, to bring us succour. Of the four vessels in which we came to Dunkirk, two escaped from this malicious attack and were grounded. Thanks be to God, I had passage on one of these ships. Many of us jumped overboard and were carried safe to land, some on boards, and some on broken pieces of the ships.

Soldiers of Medina came to my help. But the Dutch made a thousand pieces of the 270 Spaniards who came to shore from the ships which carried us from Scotland to Dunkirk. Only three of us are left alive. *"For which they are now being paid out, as beheaded"*.

From this city of Antwerp, I have written in the same manner to my Spanish friends and dated the letter October 4, 1589. I know not what happens next. As the Blessed Virgin has been with me throughout my adventures, I put my trust in her for deliverance. With this I tell the truth of the Armada and I thank the Irish Catholics for the kindly way in which you received me in your beautiful country.

Signed Francisco de Cuellar,
Captain Spanish Navy.

"Audaces Fortuna Juvat"[19]

AUTHOR'S NOTES

What is the meaning of Francisco's phrase. *"For which they are now being paid out as beheaded"?* It must refer to his two friends. Did he survive? If this were a film script, he would have returned to a hero's welcome in Spain. I should like to think he did get home to his family, if only as a reward for triumph over tragedy! However, had what occurred, I surmise we should have heard more of his Irish expedition. As it is De Cuellar left an eye-witness account of Armada and a personal diary of what happened to the unfortunate Spaniards who were shipwrecked on the shores of Ireland in 1588.

1. This was the Duke of Medina Sidonia, Don Alonso de Guzman el Bueno, Captain General of Andalusia.

2. *Zuniga,* patrona of the galleases, leader of the Naples ships, had 50 cannon, 300 rowers 400 sailors and soldiers aboard. Girona was a sister ship.

3. At that time guns could not be elevated or depressed. Accuracy depended upon steering and sailing technique. *"Wheeling About"* sent broadsides skyward and lee guns fired into the sea!

4. In 1585 an Italian engineer, Frederico Giam Belli, filled a small boat with gunpowder, reinforced the gunwale and added a clockwork timing mechanism. Sent out on a fair wind the time bomb or *'Hell Burner'* massacred a thousand Spaniards in the siege of Antwerp.

5. *San Salvador* carried much of the Armada treasure. An accidental explosion in the powder magazine blew the ship into smithereens. 250 Spaniards were burnt alive. The sea was strewn with charred bodies.

6. More than 12 ships foundered in Sligo Bay. Thousands of Spaniards were drowned. Most of those who got to shore alive were massacred by Irish peasants and English soldiers. Streedagh point is ten mile south–west of Bundoran. Various researchers suggest other dates in September.

7. The ruin of Staad Abbey is within sight of Streedagh strand. There is a chapel some 40 by 14 feet in size. St. Molaise is the local saint.

8. Cuellar always refers to adherents of the Reformed Faith as heretical Lutherians. In 1537 Henry VIII established the State Protestant Church, perhaps Staad Abbey was one of the monasteries dissolved at that time.

AUTHOR'S NOTES

9. Lough Melvin lies between Garrison (Co. Fermanagh) and Bundoran (Co. Donegal). It is named from Meilbhe who was King of Ireland for 17 years in prehistoric times.

10. It seems this village was either Glencar or Newtown.

11. Rossclougher Castle was built on a crannog. It had a circular foundation of huge boulders with very thick walls above water level. It was some 100 meters from Lough Melvin shore.

12. *"Francisco (Cuellar) (has become) more Irish than the Irish"*.

13. Sometimes a clan leader look took the title *"The"*. Queen Elizabeth ordered that "The O'Neill" must not so describe himself.

14. State papers of October 12 1588 record that the Deputy had requested 2000 additional forces. *"Sufficiently and thoroughly appointed men to direct against 3000 Spaniards"*.

15. Dunluce Castle was built c. 1300 by Richard de Burgh. In 1585 Sorley Boy MacDonnell regained it. The family retained it until 1928 when it was acquired by the Stormont Ministry of Finance.

16. Inventory of artifacts salvaged (1967-1969) shows thousands of items, mostly now in the safe keeping of the Ulster Museum. (Gold chains, rings, coins, nautical instruments, armaments, silver etc).

17. Jonathan Barton (History of Ulster) claims Castleroe as the site of this safe house. Castleroe is situated on the River Bann 2 miles south of Coleraine and 11 miles south-west of Dunluce. Nearby is a monastery founded by St. Comgall of Bangor also the Cistercian Abbey of Macosquin and Mountsandal Fort.

18. I think the *"Wretched Little Vessel"* hit the Sloch-na-Mara (whirlpool) and was fortunate to reach Rathlin Island to await favourable weather.

19. "Fortune Favours The Brave"

IV THE BLACK NUN'S LETTER

JULIA MacQUILLIN, BUNAMARGY FRIARY, C1599

Dei gratia ad te scribo. I am writing to you by the grace of God. Never have I visited the harbour of the salmon fish, as they call it, on this inhospitable north facing coast. Though often I have looked down upon the sheltered harbour and watched the salmon jumping for joy from the sea of Moyle. The poor things anticipate their return to the turbulent river which the Scotts call Bush. There is a fine view of Port Braddan from the road which leads to the chapel which Gobban built for Lassara at Templastragh – the church of the flame.[1]

I often walk the roads between the chapels of ease at Magheradonnell, Mostragee and Gracehill in Derry Keighan parish, as well as Templastragh in Billy and Drumeeny in Glenshesk. Usually I pass a pleasant hour in devotion in each chapel and then continue my solitary way, bringing spiritual food to the deserving poor, of which there are many, deserving or otherwise, in North Antrim.

However, the people at Port Braddan require no such charity. They tell me the fishermen recently settled here permanently from Scotland. Formerly they were summer visitors living in temporary accommodation during the salmon season; now they live in a grand stone built house.

From Port Braddan to my friary at Bunamargy is a good five Irish miles. Be pleased to come with me and visit our religious house. Francis,[2] the saint to whom our Order is dedicated, opened his third order to both sexes. All classes, from princes to mendicants, from the toiling artisan to the penniless widow come together to honour our patron saint. Francis teaches us *"that we must restore anything we obtain unjustly, we must reconcile ourselves to our enemies, we must keep God's commandments, we must live among the poor and minister to their necessities"*. I find it difficult to understand why the easiest of our vows to obey is the last. *"Wives must obtain their husbands permission to join the order"*. Husbands seem only too willing to obey the saints request! To keep my vows I walk the ways from Glen to Causeway, ministering to the poor and keeping God's commandments with every step. The best part of every day's journey is the return to our fine friary of Bunamargy, near the estuary of the river Margy in Glenshesk.[3]

Let me take you on a tour through our beautiful convent. The main building is our chapel. It is almost a hundred feet in length and a quarter of that in width. The side walls rise to eighteen feet, before the high pointed roof lifts our eyes and voices to our Father in heaven above. The great east window looks towards Jerusalem. It rises to seventeen feet and is almost six feet in width. I think the beautiful glass was donated by Alexander MacDonnell of Islay. He refurbished the building which was erected by the MacQuillins of the Route, in the fifteenth century. I tell you that because my name is Julia MacQuillin. Although pride is a heinous sin, I am very proud of my ancestry!

Below the window you may kneel before the high altar; please remember to make the sign of the cross. Here is the repository for our sacred relics.

Here we keep the Eucharistic vessels and our most cherished manuscripts. The cupboard is always locked securely. But as you are our special guest today, and to our guardian's delight are not staying overnight, I have obtained permission to show you the Bunamargy manuscripts.

Look and marvel at this copy of a sacred work by the blessed Thomas Aquinas[4]. There are six hundred pages on vellum. The Latin script in deep black and vivid red, is quite magnificent. It was perfected by three copyists between the years 1338 and 1340. The book belonged to the monastery of Saint Anthony of Delestmon[5]. How we obtained it for Bunamargy, I am unable to tell you. However, as our patron, Saint Francis, does not allow us to acquire goods unjustly, our Father God must have sent an angel with the book, so that we could keep it in safety in this western isle.

Now, look you here at this English translation of the Life of Christ by Cardinal Bonaventura[6]. It contains thirty five pages on vellum, two columns on each page. Here you can read about Joseph of Aramathea, one of St. Austin's sermons and some of Saint Gregory's writings.[7] Look at the last page – it reads *"this is a history of the blessed scriptures"*. The comment is signed by George Theaker. I like to think George was one of the many friends of Bunamargy and gave it to us for our edification. Often I come to read the beautiful script, although I should tell you I find the English translations much easier to understand than difficult Latin original.

Now let us continue our tour of the friary. Do you see the two doors in the south wall? That one leads into the mortuary chapel the other into our side chapel. I do not think the sunlight coming through those two windows takes away too greatly from the majesty of the great east window. I am

Bunamargy Friary

sure you agree with me. The door-way at the meeting of the east and north walls opens into our private dwelling apartments. The third door leads to the cloisters. We find this covered walk beside our gardens very convenient for ambulatory contemplation during inclement weather – the climate we enjoy for most of the year on this north coast of Ireland!

Our guardian has allowed me to take you into our private apartments. This is a very special privilege for you. I hope you will remember this as you pass the alms box! The entrance hallway runs parallel with the chapel wall, it is twenty-three feet in length, four feet wide and seven feet high. The chapel door, through which we have only now entered the hall, is accompanied by three other entrances. One opens onto the circular stone staircase of handsome construction, which leads to our dormitories on the first floor. Near to it is the entrance to the ground floor domestic rooms. The fourth door leads to the cloisters, which I have already shown to you. The smaller of the two ground floor apartments is our kitchen, some eighteen feet in length and ten feet wide. We have a practical serving hatch into the second room – our beautiful refectory. It is thirty five feet in length

The Gatehouse

and half that in width – a noble chamber with adequate doors and windows.

Now, mount with me the spiral stairway to our dormitories; only very special guests come here! The main dormitory is divided into separate chambers, each lit by its own window. At the corner of the building is the chamber of our Guardian. When special ecclesiastical guests visit Bunamargy, the guardian vacates this elegant room. Perhaps one day we shall have enough money to build a proper hospice.

As you leave our fine friary you will pass through the porter's lodge and the almonery. Here the good works of Saint Francis are achieved by our almoner, distributing alms to the sick and the poor on certain fixed days of the church year. The gatehouse is the only entrance to our well-kept grounds and gardens. The almoner's office being there in order to save the sick and the poor having to walk to the friary itself, where they might

unintentionally meet with the recluses. The room on the first floor of the gatehouse is the apartment of our porter. It is a comfortable little chamber with a fireplace where he can cook his food. He comes up to the friary only to convey messages to our Guardian. When I think about it, that chimney flue would be a safe place in which to hide our treasurers, if ever the English army descends upon us.

From the days when I was a precocious child I have been able to foresee omens of prophetic signification[8]. My parents, whom I have forsaken as our lord requires from of all his disciples, christened me with the odious name 'Julia'. They were members of the famous MacQuillin family, but now my whole family is this friary. Many people think that I am deranged and they hide in their hovels when I call to disperse Christian charity, as our founder Francis requires from his followers. Little children call me the Black Nun and even dare to throw stones in my direction. They do more harm to themselves than to me, as the angels redirect the missiles towards their peer group.

Many of my holy predictions have come to pass. Before Christmas Day in the year 1583, I told the Guardian that our beautiful chapel would become a stable. The good man thought I was preparing him for my usual request regarding decorations for the festive season. He smiled absently, in the way one does when dealing with idiots. However, I knew differently. On the ninth day of that Christmas season, the English Sir William Stanley with Captain Carleill and Captain Warrens arrived at Bunamargy. They brought a detachment of horses and foot soldiers. They set up their encampment in the friary grounds and actually stabled the horses in our chapel. The English always did consider the comfort of horses and dogs more important than human beings!

Our good friend Donnell Gorm MacDonnell came to our rescue and soon put the English to flight. Unfortunately Donnell showed little of his usual gorm on that occasion. He ordered his men to attach burning wads of cloths to their staves and ignite the dry thatch on our chapel roof. During the hour long skirmish, I am glad to tell you, several English soldiers were killed. I still recall with sorrow the incineration of seven beautiful horses in our smoke damaged chapel. Soon the roof was repaired and all things returned to normal.[9]

I predict with assured expectation that ere long Knocklayd mountain will burst open, the countryside around our friary will be flooded and the English will destroy completely our way of life. The conquest will terminate when a ship sails into the river Margy with her sails blazing on fire. I shall tell you only one other prediction; it is growing late and I must go to evening prayers. One day in the future the standing stones at Carnduff and Barnish will come together. Why this should be I know not, but I am absolutely sure it will happen.

Well now, I am very happy to have received you at my friary and I shall convey your thanks to our Guardian. Before you depart I shall answer your question about my earthly family, which I skilfully avoided during our interesting conversation. As I told you I have always resented my parents choice of the name Julia. After all, who wants to be named after a pagan Roman emperor? Furthermore, I had a pretty little sister to whom they gave a seemly Christian name. She was a silly pampered girl who always got her way and being beautiful to the depth of her skin, she was my father's favourite. He welcomed the day I became a recluse but he would not let my sister out of his senile sight. Indiscipline

Great East Window

always breeds licentiousness. My little sister became a loose stave in a well used barrel. She was with child but without husband. When her time arrived she came to me for help. Unfortunately my vows to Saint Francis would not allow me to turn her out on that miserable winter night in the year 1596, so I permitted my sibling to bed herself in my dormitory apartment. In order to parade my utter contempt for the wretchen wench, I made it clear I was going outdoors myself – where she should be – to keep my devotions.

40

While I was praying for the salvation of her soul I saw a brilliant light shining from the window of my apartment. I thought the silly strumpet had set the place on fire. I ran inside to see what further damage she had perpetrated. When I entered my room the bright light had vanished, my sister saw me and breathed her last breath sighing praise to Our Saviour. Then I remembered the similar condition of our Holy Mother Mary, forgave my little sister, and vowed to be more indulgent to lesser members of our sex than myself.

I am an old woman now, well over the three score years and ten and all is labour and sorrow, as the psalmist predicts[10]. Soon I shall be going to meet my Maker after my life of austere devotion.

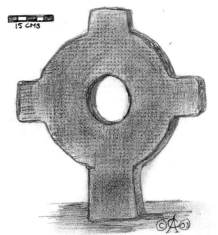

Black Nun's hole-stone cross.

The Friary Cloister

Without complaint or question, I have always allowed everyone to use me as a carpet. When I die my penance shall be that they continue to treat me in the same way. I have requested our Guardian, a silly boy only in his fifties, but kind and rather handsome – I have requested him to bury my body across the threshold of the chapel door and mark the place with a Holy Cross. Then all those who enter our beautiful sanctuary will tread on my grave and my life long humility and contrition of spirit will last till the hallowed walls of Bunamargy disintegrate with the coming of Our Lord, which second Advent I predict with complete confidence.

Be pleased to receive my blessing on your mill.

Fac Et Spera.[11]

AUTHORS NOTES

In 1536 the Irish Parliament elected Henry VIII *"Supreme Head of the Church in Ireland"*. In 1541 it conferred upon him the title *"King of Ireland"*. Henry dissolved the monasteries because *"They remained loyal to the Pope, performed superstitious ceremonies, disregarded the praise of God and the welfare of man"*.

By 1539 ninety-three Irish monasteries and friaries had been closed. Of New Years Day 1541, the North Down group was dissolved. The Irish exchequer obtained little additional revenue. However the superior monks and the friars were granted pensions, calculated on the annual income of their monasteries.

In the Gaelic parts of the island most monasteries remained undisturbed, well into the following century. Bunamargy was among these. It seems that the Rev. Patrick Hegerty was writing letters from the Friary in October 1639 and December 1640. Even as late as May 1661, the Countess of Antrim was staying in the building.

After the dissolution of Bunamargy, the Black Nun look up residence in the gate house. Perhaps it was she who removed the valuable manuscripts and secreted them in an oak chest which was found in the chimney of the gate house in 1822. When the nun died she was buried at door of the chapel, as she requested. A celtic cross marks her grave.

1.   *"Templastragh Church was built in the year 648 by St Gobban, commonly called Gobhanseir – from Gobhan, a Smith and Tsetr a carpenter. He was also a preacher of the Gospel"*. (Rev. George Hill). G. A. Birmingham suggests Gobban also built Gobhanselr's Castle near Ballycastle, probably a church, not a castle.

2.   Francis of Assisi (1182-1226) founded the Friars Minor in 1209. His approach to religion was characterised by joy, love of nature and devotion to poor and sick people.

AUTHOR'S NOTES

3.   Bun na Margy means mouth of the Margy (River). There are various spellings Bunnamairge (McCahan and Hill) Bona Margy (O.S. 1831 and McKay). Bunamargy (Shell Guide) etc. Founded c. 1500 Burnt Down, 1584, refurbished and continued in official use until 1642 and later.

4.   Thomas Aquinas (1225-1274) joined the Dominican Order in 1243. His treatises were incorporated into two Summae, in which he shows the difference between reason and faith and how they are not in conflict, but reveal God as the source of all truth.

5.   Anthony (third or fourth century) was the first Christian monastic. He founded a fraternity of ascetics in the Egyptian deserts.

6.   Bonaventura (1221-1274) was an Italian scholar of the Franciscan Order. He wrote books on the lives of Christ and St. Francis. To him God is the ultimate goal of all art, science and philosophy.

7.   Gregory (540-604) was a Benedictine monk who became Pope (590-604). He reformed monastic discipline. Gregory sent Augustine with forty monks to evangelize England. He established the liturgical musical form known as Gregorian Chant.

8.   Several of the Black Nun's predictions did come to pass. The standing stones at Carnduff and Barnish were united in the building of a new Ballycastle Harbour. She predicted the destruction of that harbour and its replacement by the present day deep sea port. In the nun's day, items were sold by size or quantity. She predicted that sale by weight would become universal with gross inflation of prices. Perhaps her best known prediction was The Antrim Coast Road, which was constructed in the 1830's. Another prediction which proved to be true was trees that would meet over the road from Ballycastle town to the sea and men would pass there in horseless carriages.

9.   Irish and English records of the attack on Bunamargy differ greatly. At this time Lord Deputy Perrot stole holy Columkill's cross from the friary chapel as a present for a lady friend (either the wife of the Secretary of State or Lady Walshyingham, the English commander's wife).

10.   Psalm 90 verse 10.

11.   Work and Hope.

V. THE PRIEST'S LETTER

PATRICK McGLAIME, PORT BRADDAN 1641

Around Port Braddan and the White Park everyone calls me "Father" - even the Protestants and Dissenters doff their bonnets with a smile. Some even leave a sack of spuds at the door of the priests house come harvest time! Later I shall tell you the reason for this happy ecumenism.[1]

My name is Patrick McGlaime, I am the priest who ministers to the few adherents of the Old Faith who still reside around the town of the north - Ballintoy.

When the English King Henry VIII ordered the dissolution of our friaries and monasteries, he did not abolish the Catholic religion and our parishes continued to operate where clergy were available.[2] In many places the parish churches were disposed, in some places the Episcopal bishop inducted Presbyterian clergy. At Bushmills my old friend Jeremiah O'Quin, was inducted as the minister of the reformed congregation.[3] Of course, this brief agape came to a sudden end when Thomas Wentworth, the one we called "Black Tom Tyrant," was appointed Lord Deputy in 1632.[4]

There have been churches at Templastragh since the time of Lassara and Gobban. These were small sally and dab structures, thatched with reeds and heather.[5] There were many salix willow trees over the country side in those days - very useful for the construction industry. Our local woodlands disappeared when Randal MacDonnell, Earl of Antrim, allowed his Scottish tenants to cut down the trees with which to build houses and make farm implements, after those days the land was cultivated.

When the Normans arrived in 1177, they taught the Irish how to build with stones. Eventually, Templastragh congregation erected a fine masonry building, some forty-seven feet in length by nineteen wide. They put up massive walls, bound by grouted lime, in some places three feet thick. These, with renovations, have withstood the tempests which whistled up from the Causeway over the centuries. Our stones did not come from the coast at Portganny. They came from the little quarry on the Croagh Road not far from Templastragh. You would think they came from the Causeway itself!

Templastragh Old Church

44

St. Gobhan's Church. Watercolour. James MacIntyre.

There is a fine window in the east gable looking towards Ballintoy. The sun pours its rising rays on our altar which is constructed of freestone, well faced and hammer dressed. Two other windows look up our lane towards the village. The door is at the west end opening towards Dunseverick Castle. The piscina is in the south wall beside the altar.[6]

Around the church we have a graveyard, generally called the Irish yard, as those of the old faith are interred therein. Some fifty yards nearer Scotland is the Scots graveyard, clinging to the verge of the sea cliffs.[7] In this yard are the foundations of an older church building. From it may well have come the slab of Derry stone engraved with the rude figure of a cross, which now lies in the ditch beside our church.

We have a priest's house. It is connected to our holy well by an elegant paved path. The straight lane leads down from Templastragh village and passes on towards the priests bray and the seashore. Down that lane in the early days of the recent rebellion the Irish herded a party of unfortunate Scottish settlers and drove them like cattle over the Gid Point, into the churning water of the murder hole. Then drunk with power, they slaughtered the women and children who had gathered for safety in the neighbouring Scull Cave.[8]

It was that tragic rebellion which brought my day of fame, quite unsought by myself. It happened shortly after what our local people call "Bloody Friday".

To my way of thinking, that atrocious rebellion and carnage is the third horrific event which shaped the history of our country. Things always come in threes.

First there was the invasion by the English King Henry, brought on as by an Irish chief and heartily commended by our Holy Father, Pope Alexander III, I am ashamed to tell you. John de Courcy brought the Sassenach Rule to our Causeway Coast in 1177 and tried to force on us a way we did not want to go.[9]

Stewart Memorial, Ballintoy Church.

46

Then in the early years of the seventeenth century came the Plantation of Ulster, after our leaders had made the countryside a wilderness and escaped to enjoy papal pensions in Rome. We lost our good farmland to the settlers.[10]

The third tragedy is the rebellion of 1641, which devastated the countryside once again, and only now has been laid to rest.

The Rebellion, happened this way, as usual for three reasons! First Rory O'More's plot to seize Dublin Castle in February 1641 to *Defend King Charles and Restore "The Faith"* - he was last seen fleeing to Bofin Island disguised as a fisherman. Then there was a plot inaugurated by the disbanded officers of Black Tom's army, after his execution in May 1641. The third plot came from Sir Phelim O'Neill M.P., who sided with Rory O'More and then disappeared to another island hideout in Tyrone among the bushes.

Our local folk did not give a fig that the conspirators were debt-written gentry who had benefited from the plantation and feared a Puritan administration in England. For us it was a statement against the Scottish settlers who had seized our farms and consigned us to the glens and bogs.[11]

One sabbath morning in Dervock church Archibald Stewart of Ballintoy Castle, Lord Antrim's agent, told the congregation that insurrection had come upon the Route and soon would overwhelm all of us on the north coast.

As his Lordship's land agent, Archibald Stewart was responsible for the defence of the area. Soon a regiment was recruited. Foolishly Archibald gave command of two companies to Tirlough O'Cahan of Dunseverick and Allaster McColl MacDonnell, both of whom turned against the government forces when the battle commenced.

At the turn of the year 1642, the Irish were assembling to cross the river Bann into County Antrim. Commander Stewart marched the north coast regiment to Port Naw.

On the night of 2nd January 1642 O'Cahan and MacDonnell deserted, murdered some of their fellow officers and joined with the rebels. The Irish crossed the river Bann marched victoriously on Ballymoney, slaughtering all the settlers they could find between the river and the town. The massacre continued in the streets of Ballymoney town.

Flushed with success and blood lust the rebels marched on Coleraine. Meanwhile Commander Stewart assembled a second regiment from the remnant of his first army. He met the rebels at Laney on the Coleraine Road.

Stewart's army was completely routed. Six hundred men were massacred, less than three hundred escaped in disorganised retreat. That dark day became known as Black Friday. It was Friday, 11th February 1642.

Now the rebels turned their vengeance on Coleraine, Dunluce and Ballintoy Castles, then on Ballycastle town. The road from Ballymoney was strewn with the corpses of children, their mothers and their sisters.

The outnumbered garrison of Ballintoy Castle heard of the burning of Dunluce, saw the red glow on the night sky, feared for their lives and the safety of their bairns and wives. Surrender would mean annihilation. They stood firm, repelled every assault and cheered when the enemy turned tail and retreated in the direction of Ballycastle.

I may tell you it was all Archibald Stewart could do to keep his volunteers within the castle walls -

the family men beseeched the commander sally forth and attack the foe, so that they could defend their kith and kin.

I got word to the soldiers that they need not worry, their loved ones were safe within the castle chapel. The women and children filled the place a lot better than they did on a Sabbath morning.

Our Irish commander James MacDonnell had more generosity than his fellows. He allowed me to take water to the terrified refugees in the Ballintoy Church. What else could I do to save them? How could I relieve their hunger? I knew I would be searched before each visit to the thirsty prisoners. The water vessels I brought were deep. I filled them with oatmeal, leaving a few inches of clear water on the top!

Had I been caught the bairns would not have lived to tell this tale and I should have been killed like any settler. Thus the captives survived until the Irish army marched on to Ballycastle and eventually government help came for the relief of Ballintoy Castle.

That was my simple act of mercy. The settlers never let me forget my day of fame.

Now let me tell you how the rebellion came to an end. At Ballycastle, Alice O'Neill, Dowager Countess of Antrim, had been informed of the intended visit of the Irish army to her town. On the approach of the rebel soldiers the English and Scots inhabitants rushed to the Countess for protection, within the castle walls. Lady Alice selected those trades people she considered necessary for the convenience of the castle and the life-style to which she and her daughter were accustomed. Then she ordered the servants to throw the rest to the rebels who barbarously murdered them before the castle gates.

General Robert Monro was dispatched to settle the Irish question. Monro's Scots met Owen Roe O'Neill's six thousand Hibernians at Benburb on the Blackwater. The date was the sixth of June in the year 1646. The British army were trounced, losing some three thousand men.

Then the butcher Oliver Cromwell arrived on the fifteenth of August 1649 with an army of twenty thousand, a navy and much first class artillery. He ravaged the country. In our area he destroyed Dunseverick Castle and executed the O'Cahan. But all that is another story.

Those were terrible times. One winter night, many years later sitting around the fire in the house at Port Braddan, we recalled the year of forty two. Archibald Stewart told us of his friends who were killed in the church of Ramoan. He declared Ballintoy's fortune in having a priest of the old faith. Edmund O'Haggan, a servant of the old Countess of Antrim, told us what happened at Ballycastle, tears in his dim eyes. Coll MacAllister, who hails from Derry Keighan, described the massacre of the seven hundred British soldiers slain on black Friday. He was in Laney that very day.

It took many years for the country to settle down, which it did as it always does with the passage of time.

Pax Vobiscum [12]

48

AUTHOR'S NOTES

"Tradition states that this truly Good Samaritan was called Priest MacGlaime, but nothing is known of him save this one noble Christian act.- it is quite enough to consecrate his memory to the latest posterity - to preserve his name in everlasting remembrance" (George Hill).

"About the end of the eighteenth century the vestry of Ballintoy Church voted parochial relief to a poor man named McGlaime, because he was a relative of the priest" (Hugh Alexander Boyd).

1. "This humanity and praiseworthy act of Priest McGlaim was not forgotten. In consideration thereof not only have the McGlaims been respected and patronised by their Protestant brethren, but the poor of that name have been liberally relieved from the funds of the aforesaid church". (Ordnance Survey Memories. August 13, 1838).

2. The King rejected papal authority in the question of divorce but wished to preserve Catholic belief. Indeed he considered himself Defender of the Faith. (Conferred by Pope Leo X in 1521; confirmed by Parliament in 1544). More than half of the Irish monasteries remained undisturbed. Superiors who received early retirement got pensions calculated on the annual ministerial income (£6 to £50). Ordinary monks and friars received £1 to £3.

3. Rev. Jeremiah O'Quin, M.A. was the first minister to serve the parish of Billy after the Reformation. He was a Roman Catholic by birth, a graduate of Glasgow University, and the first Irishman to be ordained to the Presbyterian Ministry in Ireland. He was a fluent speaker in Irish and spent some time in the west preaching the Gospel in the native tongue. His grave is in Billy churchyard

4. King Charles I appointed Thomas Wentworth (later Earl of Stafford) Lord Deputy in 1632. He forced the clergy to discard the Articles of 1615 and conform to Anglican practice.

5. Upright stakes were inserted into the ground and interlaced with branches. Layers of clay were built up on this support to provide strong sun baked walls.

6. A piscina is a perforated stone basin, set into a wall, used to carry away water after rinsing the chalice. It is the lower part of a fenestella - a wall-niche set to the south of the altar. The upper part of the fenestella is a credence - a shelf on which the eucharistic elements are placed before consecration. One remains in the ruins of the Templastragh Church to the present way.

7. In burial the Scottish settlers may have wished to get as near as possible to their homeland. Formerly the Ecclestical lands were in the possession of the Lesley family of Ballymoney. Today they are supervised by Moyle District Council. Several local families continue to use the Templastragh grave yard.

8. The O.S. Memoirs (fair sheets by Thomas Fagan April to August 1838) refers to skull cave "so called in consequence of several skulls and other human bones having been found there, supposed to be those who took refuge during the 1641 war who were discovered and murdered there. Opposite the cave is a deep pit in the edge of the sea called the murder hole. It is said that here numbers of persons were

AUTHOR'S NOTES

thrown into the sea at the same period. The Archaeologist's letter refers to the same cave.

9. The ring of castles along the Causeway Coast enforced a servile rule on the Irish people. (i.e. Norman Feudal Rule). Irish life-style operated on a system where each person was important as a member of the tribal family.

10. The Flight of the Earls. O'Neill (Tyrone) O'Donnell (Tryconnell) and Maguire (Fermanagh), fearing government action, sailed from Rathmullen (4 September 1607) to Rome, where they lived on Papal pensions. Their confiscated lands became available for plantation.

11. The settlers took the best agricultural lands. The native Irish were driven into the Glens of Antrim. Some of the above historical points appear in the author's notes to other letters in the book. As each letter should have the ability "To stand on its own two feet", I have included the references as they are directly connected to the Priest's story. Whenever information is reported in the author's notes after each letter, I have attempted to approach the subject from a different perception in each case.

12.   Peace be with you.

VI A LETTER FROM A DUCHESS

LADY CATHERINE MANNERS, DUCHESS OF BUCKINGHAM, DUNLUCE. 1649

Greetings to you from Waterford, where I am abed with sickness and have much time to write of happier days. I shall tell you my story and especially of those days I spent in that draughty, cold and isolated Dunluce Castle, around the coast from your little mill house. I remember well pretty Port Braddan of the jumping fish. I served my guests many a fine Port Braddan salmon, before my cook and her kitchen fell off my castle into the turbulent Atlantic Ocean in 1639.

You will know me as Catherine Manners. My father was the 22nd Lord Roos, Baron Hamlake, the 6th Earl of Rutland. My brothers, Henry and Francis, both died of the effects of witchcraft., while they were strapping youngsters. I was abused by the same diabolical agency. However, I wish to say nothing of it but that it made me very careful of people for the rest of my life.[1]

Nevertheless, I had a highly privileged childhood, as we are one of the richest families in England. I was educated in the Roman Catholic faith and inherited my family's immense possessions.

In 1620 I became the more than willing bride of young George Villiers. Let me tell you of my first husband.

George was an extraordinary youth, whose remarkable good looks, gracefulness and sheer becomingness, heaped honours and fame upon him. These he accepted with a nonchalance which rendered him even more attractive! He was the younger son of Sir George Villiers of Brookesly in Leicester, by a second marriage into the Beaumont family. After an education in the Reformed Faith, while still in his teens, his mother sent him to France for three years. This was to learn the language of the Court, to acquire skilled equestrianism and to win expertise in the dance; for all of which that foreign Court was famous. He surpassed all the young English gallants on this return to England, at the age of twenty one years, truly *"Le Beau Ideal"*.

I well remember the first day George appeared at the Court of King James. The stomach of every lady, young and old, churned to fainting; our legs trembled so much that some sat down, even in the presence of the King. The sighings and fannings were frantic. Never in a man had I seen such a handsome face and lithe physique demanding female attention!

All eyes turned to King James as George approached for presentation and audience. His majesty was most delighted. He always liked *"Bonny Boys"* as he quipped, especially when they were *"well groomed for viewing"*. At that time His Majesty was tiring of his current favourite, the Earl of Somerset. Soon George, completely without intention, made himself gracious and indispensable to the King, whose disposition was flowing in affection to his new cosset. We had not seen His Majesty take to anyone so completely as he did to George Villiers. King James nicknamed him *"Stennie"* after a fancied resemblance to a picture of Saint Stephen in the royal collection.

Within the week George became the King's cup

Manor House in Dunluce Castle.

bearer. Being so recently returned from the French court, his knowledge of affairs and fashions surpassed anyone in London. The bright new opinions and conversation he brought to table amused the royal person with the sort of entertainment he enjoyed most at mealtime.

The position of cupbearer lasted but a few weeks. The King knighted George, so that he could become a gentleman of the bedchamber and equerry-in-waiting upon every royal request. Promotion followed to knight of the Order of the Garter, for services rendered. This boon was solely in the King's gift and made George one of the twenty-five most important courtiers. Mon Dieu, how my intestines groaned when first I saw George wearing the dark blue garter on his left leg, the velvet mantle lined with white silk, the crimson hood and grand collar of the premier Order of State. He was magnificent!

Of course, the rapid elevation made many jealous enemies at court, for which neither George or the King gave a fig. Royal preference did not end there. In rapid succession George became a Baron, then a Viscount at the age of twenty-four, an Earl the following year and a Marquis in 1618,

St. Cuthbert's Church, Dunluce.

when he was only twenty-six. Such meteoric success has never been seen before or since at Court.

George was most courteous to me, as he was to everyone, in the palace and elsewhere. Although I threw myself at him on every possible occasion, he never favoured me with any special attention. Then in 1620, when he had become Lord High Admiral of England, George asked my father if he might pay me court. He did not conceal the fact that he was as much in love with my immense fortune as he was with my wit and beauty! My father, equally in love with his position at court, rejected objections to my necessary espousal of the Reformed Faith and rapidly gave his blessing.

I came to George heart and soul, with a dowry of £20,000 and an income of £8,000. We were married in a closed room at the Chapel Royal by Bishop Withers, our witnesses being His Majesty and my father. The ceremony was consummated within the hour and within nine months our first child was born!

George became Lord Warden of the Cinque Ports, Master of the Horse and every office of state in the Kingdoms of England, Scotland and Ireland you can quote. In 1623 the King ennobled us as the Duke and Duchess of Buckingham.

Never did any of these great offices change my husband even one whit. He served the throne to his best ability, showed courtesy to everyone and thought the best even of his enemies.

My husband looked after the interests of our two families - the Villiers and the Rutlands. This aroused *"Jalousie de Metier"* among our peers, who saw the expenses of state so vast that the prospect of poverty was predicted. Indeed, afterwards such did befall the Crown, almost to the ruin thereof.

So it was no great wonder to me that my beloved

husband was murdered in 1628, being then only thirty six years of age.[2] We had eight ecstatic years together. As I look back over the twenty succeeding years, here on my sick bed in Irish Waterford, I should have had it no other way. Men like my Buckingham were not born to grow old and ugly. To me he is as beautiful today as the day he first appeared in the court of King James.

60 cms

Port Saint Anne's Cannon

Let me tell you of that day when my heart stopped beating and my only wish was to join my murdered husband. It happened thus. I was in conversation with my good friend the Countess of Anglesey. I remember we were walking on the gallery of a house in Portsmouth, number 10, the High Street. It was about ten o'clock in the morning. A curtain was pulled back, a door opened and my husband with other gentlemen came into the hall from the parlour. They were going to their coaches to have audience with the King, who was residing at about four miles distance.

As we looked down into the hall, a frenzied lieutenant of the army, John Felton, threw a blow with a tenpenny dagger knife. I beheld the blood of my dearest love gushing from him. That gruesome scene returns in dreams, even after all these years. No prince of any realm ever manifested a more lively regret for the loss of a faithful servant than did His Majesty for my Lord George, Duke of Buckingham.

My husband's misfortune was that he had no close friend who would advise him independently, although I tried often enough! He was a just, candid, liberal and generous friend to the King and the best husband that ever lived.

The years of grieving passed and by 1635 my natural yearnings for a husband started to reawaken, as I was yet a young and unsatisfied woman. Young Randal MacDonnell appeared at the court of King Charles and all the old *affaires de coeur* erupted. It was a *déjà vu*. In two ways only was Randal like George, fantastically handsome and with the body of a Greek god. I could not wait to have him with me in my bed.

Randal comes from your part of the Kingdom, indeed your mill at Port Braddan lies within our extensive Antrim estates. In 1620 Randal had become the Lord Dunluce when only a boy of ten. He succeeded to the Earldom of Antrim when he was twenty seven, and came to Court.

The Antrim family instructed all their clan members in the Highland Way - which he told me was *"Redshanks Schooling"*. He said *"Summer and winter we went bare bums and bare legs. We spent every day, sunshine or snow, hunting red deer, wolves and foxes with our hands. Then we went running, leaping and swimming in the ice cold water. For sport we were always throwing and shooting darts. I wore neither hat, cap, shoe nor stocking till I was well over eight years of age".* Randal was educated in the Catholic Faith. My mother-in-law, Lady Alice,[3] sent him to the continent to polish the rough learning he had acquired in Ireland.

The MacDonnells of Antrim were an ancient family, having been keepers of the Stone of Scone[4]. Randal swept me off my feet, much to the displeasure of many a courtier who saw me as an available heiress either for themselves or their sons. Randal showed little interest in the inheritance I brought to him[5], except to get rid of it as quickly as possible! He was pathetically pleased that I wanted to be his wife and that I was willing to rejoin the Catholic Church.

For some time we lived in great splendour in Buckingham House at Chelsea in London. My father-in-law, First Earl of Antrim died on December 10, 1636. Randal became the second Earl and inherited Dunluce Castle with all its furniture and chattles. His brother Alexander received Glenarm Castle.

There were many at court extremely envious of Randal's good fortune and our matrimonial happiness. Our chief antagonist was that odious little man Thomas Wentworth. King Charles had appointed him Lord Deputy in Ireland. His aim was to fleece the Irish and force the Protestant Church on the people. At court, arrogantly he demolished anyone who contradicted him. We did with vehemence! Randal thought we had better go over to County Antrim for a while, in order to find what we could do to salvage the King's honour.

And so we came to take up residence at Dunluce Castle, more or less neighbours to your beautiful White Park Bay. Randal had boasted to me of his Irish castle, its wild magnificent beauty and how the sea birds flew backwards past the windows on a stormy day! Nothing prepared me for the house I was to find at the end of that tedious journey from London to the Causeway Coast. Let me tell you of my first romantic Irish castle.

Dunluce was built by the Anglo-Normans, a quarter of a millennium before the fine spring day on which I got my first sight of the awesome pile. It looked its full age that day, even though it had been refurbished with funds gleaned from a Spanish Armada ship which was wrecked on the razor cruel rocks one hundred feet below.[6]

The castle had been erected on an island "dun" in the north Atlantic ocean and it is approached by a terrifying draw bridge. On the mainland side of the bridge there is a pretty little Irish town and a good church.[7] The wild winds are not so withering on that side of the chasm, so I attempted to make a garden there, much to the amusement of the servants, but with their ever loyal support.

The castle has tall circular towers and a gate house with finely corbelled bartizans from which the draw bridge operated. Within the upper yard there is a comfortable two-storey manor-house, with grand bay windows to catch the westering sun. At some time there had been a sheltered loggia, unfortunately part of it had been converted into a smart parlour. The servants quarters were in the lower yards with the bake house and a multitude of little offices, which I never entered. And there also was the famous kitchen!

In 1639, when one of the customary hurricanes was blasting the castle cliffs, our kitchen actually tumbled down into the Atlantic ocean! With it went our cooks, table servants and the dinner. Only the castle tinker was saved as an eye witness. He had been sitting in a window embrasure, mending pots and pans.

The castle was full of guests at that time. We were looking forward to dinner when a thunderous roar rent the air and the whole dining hall shook under us. *Mon Dieu,* what if the whole castle had hurtled down the cliffs into the sea on that momentous evening? I vowed to Randal I would not spend another night on that infernal rock. Later I was told some of the servants set fire to their hall to make sure I should never return. I hope that was from love for us, rather than they preferred the castle to themselves!

That night we removed to our agent's house at Ballymagarry[8] and later to our brother Alexander's castle at Glenarm where we were made most welcome.[9] We crossed the sea to Oxford for a time, where the King was in residence. Then we returned to Ireland to live in Dublin, where Randal took his seat in the Irish House of Lords.[10] Randal's father had to resign the Antrim seat in 1634, being ill. The first Earl was accounted the best of men. He was a just, generous, merciful and indulgent member of Parliament. Randal wished to follow in his father's footsteps. Unfortunately, that was not to occur.

The stupidity of Thomas Wentworth and Archbishop Laud in dealing with those kind Irish people, whom they neither understood nor even wanted to know, provoked a common rising. We were in Dublin when it came to a head on October 23, 1641. Randal and I fled to my sister-in-law's residence at Slane.[11]

Our enemies shouted to the rooftops that we had joined the Irish Party. This was completely untrue, as my husband had avoided all identification with the rebels.

The King pronounced Randal innocent of the origin of the rebellion. Of course this angered our friends in the Irish Party. I soon found that it is impossible to straddle an Irish fence!

From Slade we were forced to remove to Maddenstowne[12] and there remained for many weeks until April 5, 1642, when occurred that importance battle at Kilrush[13]. We did all in our power to assist the wounded of both parties.

After the battle my husband thought it was too dangerous for me to stay in Ireland. He sent me to my family in England for safety. I did not wish to leave his side at this difficult time but he was adamant. *Mon Dieu,* how I missed the man. He had a couple of pet names for me *"My Good Woman"* and when he was feeling particularly amorous *"Papps"*. It was at this time that I commissioned a full sized painting, seated and surrounded by my three children. It is a very fine picture even though I say so myself. Randal deeply appreciates that early birthday present.[14]

After I had departed for England, Randal went north to Coleraine. He helped the suffering citizens, under siege from the Irish party, to get use of the Liberties for grazing their animals.[15] Randal reached Dunluce Castle on April 28, and successfully alleviated the hardships of our people on the Causeway Coast.

Despite all this, when Robert Monro, like a bat out of hell, arrived at Dunluce the following June, he took great joy in bombarding our castle. Without warrant or cause he tried to destroy the old place, plundered our treasures and misappropriated the rents of our estates. Worst of all that devil Monro imprisoned my husband in Joymount House at Carrickfergus, which detention lasted from June to December.[16]

Fortunately Randal has many friends! His servants obtained a pass for a sick man, and carried Randal on a stretcher out of Joymount House to freedom, without rousing suspicious. A ship was arranged to carry him from Carrickfergus to Holyhead, thence to Oxford for a conference with Queen Henrietta Maria. Her Majesty was keen to meddle in the affairs of state and convinced us that Randal could bring peace to Ireland. Before this royal visit he came to see me, still disguised as a sick man. We had grand laughter together, for I did not recognise my Randal until half an hour of the clock has passed by!

A week or so later, His Majesty ordered my husband to return to Ireland. The King's armies were being reduced to great distress, so Randal brought letters from the King to James, Marquis of Ormonde: *"Cessation of arms with the Confederate Irish is an absolute necessity"*.

Randal requisitioned the first boat available and crossed to Newcastle in the County Down. A messenger was sent ashore to discover if the castle was in friendly hands. This scout was to reply by flying his shirt from a stick. Unfortunately Monro's soldiers captured the messenger and flew the friendly flag! Randal went ashore only to be recaptured and returned to Carrickfergus to serve nine months imprisonment.

Again our friends contrived a cunning rescue. In October, Captain George Gordon concealed a coil of rope in his breeches, conveyed it his prisoner and thus assisted Randal to escape from custody.[17]

Monro persured my husband to Glenarm Castle and from thence to the glen to which he had fled for safety. In the glen our loyal groom Maconkey exchanged clothes and horse with Randal. When Monro's soldiers appeared, man and master went in different directions. The soldiers followed the substitute Lord Antrim, while Randal escaped to Kilkenny, to serve both King and Church.[18]

When I had been obliged to leave my husband for safety in 1642, first I went to York to stay at Court for ten days. On July 11 that year I decided to return to my old home at Belvoir in Leicestershire, where I had much time to concern myself with worry for my husband's safety and cares for our properties in Ireland.

One day George Digby[19] drew to my attention that the law of wardship. As regards Irish Catholics, is most oppressive. He told me that the heirs of Catholic noblemen can be cheated out of their rightful estates. I asked Digby to arrange that the wardship of our nephew, Lord Slain be granted to me personally. However, it was pointed out that such an arrangement would cause great scandal to my husband. Regretfully, I agreed that the wardship be granted in the name of Mister Pearce Moore, a good Irish Protestant. Such restrictions on Catholics and Dissenters, who make up the majority of our people at Dunluce, should be abolished by King Charles.

At that time I was resting at Pendennis, the fashionable watering place on the western side of Falmouth Bay.[20] I had not been in my usual good health for some time and I always enjoyed the Pendennis pleasure garden, especially in the splendid summer sunshine of July 1644.

By that time the political cockpit has moved to England. Two summers before, the King had set up his standard at Nottingham. A high wind blew it down the same night - an aupice of what was to come! The battle of Marston Moore[21] convinced us that we should be safer in Ireland. In January of that year Randal had been created the first Marquis of Antrim[22]. It was full time to go home together.

As I told you, that Devil Monro had ransacked our castle at Dunluce. Because of the recent uprising none of our houses was suitable for occupation. Thomas Butler offered us the use of his castle near Carrick-on-Suir,[23] but I preferred to be under no obligation to the tenth, or any other Earl of Ormond. We chose to live privately at Wexford, Waterford, Kilkenny and Clonmel, wherever I could be nearest to my husband.

As soon as we arrived here at Waterford, I fell ill again. A few nights ago, I dreamed of the family curse which had taken both my brothers. I knew I was not long for this world and Randal became very worried. He wrote to James Ormond begging that Dr. Fennell would come to visit me. I was amused at his trust and faith, especially when he wrote the word "Haste" in very large letters on the envelope.

I am quite sure Dr. Fennell can do nothing for me. I am content to go to meet my Maker. I have enjoyed an exciting life and the love of the two most handsome men in the world. My only regret is that I leave no seed of the Antrim family. I pray, if God wills, that Randal will find another "Good Woman" who can birth the second Marquis of Antrim.

I am using these last days writing to my family, and to my dear Irish and English friends - and not least this to you on that isolated Causeway Coast, overlooking the cold Atlantic ocean, where Randal and I experienced such interesting occasions.

Tourjours Pret.[24]

30 CMS.

18th. century cannon.

AUTHORS NOTES

Catherine Manners, Duchess of Buckingham, Lady wife of Randal, second Earl and first Marquis of Antrim, died at Waterford in November 1649 and was buried there. The Villiers monument is in Westminster Abbey, on the north side of the tomb of Henry VIII. Effigies of the Duke and Duchess lie on a table supported by eight emblematical figures. Catherine's wish that her second husband would remarry was fulfilled. In 1653 Randal married Rose O'Neill, daughter of Sir Henry O'Neill of Shanes Castle, alas they did not produce offspring. His brother Alexander became the third Earl of Antrim.

1. Punishment for witchcraft was rife throughout Europe at this time. In 1563 (Elizabeth) it became a capital offence, reinforced in 1603 (James I). In 1711 nine people from Islandmagee, Co. Antrim, were imprisoned and pilloried, In England and Wales all acts were repealed in 1736; in Ireland not until 1821.

2. August 23, 1628.

3. Wealthy Lady Alice (Ellis) O'Neill, the daughter of Hugh, Earl of Tyrone, married the first Earl of Antrim in 1604. She fled from Ballycastle Manor during the 1641 rebellion, losing her jewels. She appeared before Cromwell's courts in Coleraine. Lady Alice died after her eightieth birthday in 1663.

4. Tradition relates this was the crowning stone of the kings of Dal Riata, preserved for that purpose at Dunseverick Castle. The clan Mac Donnell was its keeper. For political reasons Fergus removed it to Scone on the foundation of Argyle (Eastern Gael). Scone (Perth Shire) became the Scottish capital, where the kings were crowned. It was removed by Edward I in 1297, and is incorporated in the coronation chair at Westminster Abbey.

5. Catherine had brought to her first husband George Villiers £20,000 in hand and £8,000 a year.

6. A cave goes through the rock under the castle (250m) which served as a secret entry and escape route. A souterrain indicates habitation of the Dun long before the Anglo-Norman conquest (1177). The Antrim family deserted the castle after the 1641 rebellion and it fell to decay. What remained on the rock was acquired for preservation by the N.I. government in 1928 as an ancient monument. The mainland buildings were taken into care in 1971..

7. The town of Dunluce lay on the mainland opposite the castle rock. During the Irish rebellion (1641) it was destroyed and the settlers sent home to Scotland. Some moved to found a fishing village at Portrush. St. Cuthbert's church (said to be ruinous, in the 1622 Ulster Visitation) was refurbished when Catherine came to the castle. Its splendid roof was moved to a local barn, when the congregation removed to Bushmills in 1821.

AUTHOR'S NOTES

8. Ballymagarry house seems to have been the agent's residence, (John Macnaghten). The gardens supplied provisions for the castle. After the Restoration, a fine unfortified house was built, rather than repairing the castle. It was destroyed by fire in 1750 and a grand new mansion erected nearby in the style of a French chateau.

9. Randal's brother Alexander had inherited Glenarm. Their father had started to build this hunting-lodge in 1603 and continued to make additions until his death in 1636. Originally the site was a Bisset castle (mid-13th century) which was tumbled in 1597. The Crown Grant to the first Earl required him to build houses in each of the Baronies. Dunluce, Glenarm, Dunaynie and Clough Castles.

10. June 17th 1640.

11. Slane Castle, County Meath, about 24 miles from Dublin. Lady Anne MacDonnell, Randal's sister, married William Fleming, nineteenth baron Slane.

12. Maddenstown was the residence of Randal and Catherine's friend, the Earl of Castlehaven. It is near the Curragh, 2 miles south of Kildare.

13. In the battle of Kilrush, April 5, 1642, the Irish party was trounced by Government forces.

14. Francis Anne Vane, Marchioness of Londonderry and daughter of Anne Catherine, Countess of Antrim, built Garron Tower in 1848. Here she assembled many Antrim family treasures, among these was the painting of the Duchess. A portrait in the Government Art Collection (GAC 2174 "Family of George Villiers, 1st Duke of Buckingham) was purchased from Sotheby's on 29 June 1953, and is ascribed to the Circle of Van Dyck. The Garron Tower sale took place about 1930. The painting is reproduced on the website of the Department for Culture, Media and Sport. (www.gac.culture.gov.uk). The children in the painting are the family by Catherine's first husband.

15. The Liberties. James I granted everything within a radius of three Irish miles from the centre of Coleraine to be within the jurisdiction and liberty of the town.

16. Joymount House seems to have been used as a barracks at this time. The palace was built by Sir Arthur Chichester. It had 365 windows, a turreted gate house, a court and a terrace. Possibly by Inigo Jones, it extended to 35 meters. Impossible to upkeep, the family vacated it in 1724, the house was demolished in 1768.

AUTHOR'S NOTES

17. It seems Captain George Gordon was the Earl of Sutherland's brother. He married Lady Rose MacDonnell, Randal's sister. Later he was promoted to the rank of Lieut. Colonel.

18. At Kilkenny the Supreme Council (Confederated Catholics of Ireland) pressed Randal to take the oath. (here in brief) *"I promise to defend the true Roman Catholic religion against all who would oppose it. I swear allegiance to our Sovereign Lord King Charles, his heirs and successors and to defend the regal government and will punish all who do contrary to this oath."*

19. George Digby was the second Earl of Bristol. Lord Slane was Randal's nephew, Lady Anne MacDonnell having married William Fleming, Baron Slane. The iniquitous law of wardship against Irish Catholics was introduced by James I. One clause of it required that wards be brought up in the college near Dublin, in English habits and religion.

20. July, 1644.

21. The great royalist defeat at Marston Moor, Newcastle, England, July 1644.

22. King Charles conferred the title of Marquis on Randal by privy seal dated at Oxford on January 26, 1644. Fee of £40 per annum issuing from customs of the port of Coleraine.

23. Carrick was considered the best example of an Elizabethan mansion in Ireland.

24. Tourjours prez - Always prepared. The motto of the MacDonnell's of Antrim

---

VII   A LETTER FROM AN IRISH GENTLEMAN

GILLDUFF O'CAHAN. DUNSEVERICK 1657

You will know me as Gillduff O'Cahan, last of the Route branch of the clan O'Cahan of Dunseverick. My father, Giolla Dubh O'Cahan and my beloved brother were cruelly beheaded by the English at Carrickfergus Castle in 1653. I was the last member of my family to live at Dunseverick, before our home was destroyed by the soldiers of that devil Cromwell and then confiscated by the English government.[1]

To the east of our castle lies the little bay of Port Braddan and its sibling harbour at Port Moon in the west. There my family was wont to buy sea salmon to warm the bellies of the guests who came to the great banquets for which our castle was famous in days long gone. The few remaining ruins are but an Irish mile along the fishermen's path from Port Braddan. So, as you live at the peaceful little harbour of the leaping salmon, walk around to the castle after I tell you something of the rise and fall of Dunseverick and the House of O'Cahan.

King Sobhairce first erected defences on the Causeway Coast in the year of the world 3668.[2] In front of the castle dun spread forth the Feigh, the level grounds on which the clans assembled every spring season. There they brought honour to our leaders, with celebrations in bright carnival and contest in bold athletic prowess.

Sobhairce lived on the dun and nurtured his family until AM 3707, when he was killed by Eochaidh Meanin – a clan from Northern Europe which had settled on the islands which you can see clearly over the sea to the north of Dunseverick.[3]

Some four and a half centuries later we know that Roitheachtaigh, Lord of Dunseverick was struck down by a lightening bolt during one of the great storms which sweep along our inhospitable coast in winter time. This good leader held the distinction of being the first man in Ireland to drive a chariot with four horses.

Then in the fourth century before Christ came the horrific incineration of the castle. The people of the north owned the famous Bull of Cooley. This amazing animal possessed the human power of knowledge. The queen of Connaught, Maeve, was jealous and could not sleep peacefully in her bed till the bull sired her favourite cow. The warrior queen must have a calf by the bull of Cooley! The keepers of the bull could not be cajoled into parting with the precious semen sperm.

Long did the Queen coax and wheedle without the success to which she was accustomed. Finally, the perfidious woman invaded Ulster with her warriors to satisfy her taurine yearning. Cuchulainn was defeated in the famous battle which he fought single handed and Maeve's fantasy was satisfied.[4]

Many are the tales told of this bovine epic. Let me tell you what I think is the truth of the matter. Perhaps, it was a poetic allegory concerning the unrequited amor of a frustrated amazon for the handsome and bull-like Cuchulainn of Ulster. However that may be, the rejected Queen Maeve

The Children of Lir. Oil. 20" x 20".

torched Dunseverick castle before she returned to her western dominions with a harem of fifty Ulster colleens.

In Anno Domini 30, Conal Cearnac of Dunseverick witnessed the crucifixion of Jesus Christ in Jerusalem. It happened this way. Conal was champion of the Red Branch Knights of Ulster.

The Knights were invited to the greater British island to test their acclaimed strength against the Roman Army securocrats, who were ruling England at that time. Conal defeated all the Roman champions in wrestling, jumping and throwing the weight. The Romans were heartily impressed by the valour of the Ulsterman and honoured Conal with an invitation to Rome to pit his strength against the greatest gladiator of the Empire. Of course, Conal won the famous wrestling match over which Caesar Augustus presided, and presented the Ulsterman with the victor's crown of palm leaves.

Conal became a celebrity with the Roman soldiers and continued his grand tour of the Empire, arriving at Jerusalem on the day of the crucifixion of our Lord Jesus Christ.

As yet, Christianity had not reached the shores of Ireland, nor had Conal heard of the peaceful way of Jesus. He was standing near the foot of the cross when Longinus thrust his spear into Christ's side. Drops of water and blood fell on Conal's brow and thus he was baptised; the first Irishman to receive the sacred blood and body of Our Lord.

Conal's military friends said *"come take your chance and throw a dice for this fine seamless robe, it could be your trophy to take back to Hibernia"*. Conal won the prize but he would not accept the seamless robe. So touched was he when he heard the story of Jesus, that he stayed with the soldiers till the body was taken down from the cross. It was Conal's strong shoulders which pushed aside the stone from the mouth of the sepulchre cave when Joseph of Arimathea placed the body in the tomb.[4]

Conal Cearnac brought home the good news of the Gospel to the Causeway Coast. And so it was that Saint Patrick made Dunsererick fort his local domicile when he came to North Antrim.

About the year 450 our patron saint travelled slighe Miodhluachra, the road to the north. Like the spokes of a wheel, Irish roads spread out from the hub at Tara.[6] He visited Dunseverick, blessed the castle and our well at the foot of the cliff.[7] While at Dunseverick Saint Patrick ordained Olcan to the See of Armoy, which later became the Diocese of Connor.

Olcan had been a posthumous infant. It seems Darius, the local chieftain of Armoy, heard the forlorn crying of a child coming from the recently infilled grave of a young girl. Quickly he opened the grave and found a living child beside the deceased mother.

The boy was given to Patrick who celebrated the sacrament of Baptism. As there were neither parents nor god parents, Patrick himself vouched for Olcan's nurture in the Christian faith. After some years the local man became the bishop in the local church at Arhir Muy.[8]

A couple of centuries later the O'Cahan of Dunseverick invited Gobban to encourage the people of the north coast in the Way of Christ. A folk tale tells how he built many churches around Templastragh, one of which was in your hamlet at Port Braddan.

We had a murder at the fort in the year 664. Eochaidh Iarliathe, King of Ulster was cruelly slain in revenge for an evil deed done by his daughter. She had married Ronan, the King of Leinster! Eochaidh was buried in Connor grave yard. We still have the dirge words of his bard, the poet Flaithir.

"This day distinguished the grave of Eochaidh in the earth of the church of Conneire, which has received the great heat of his mouth. Slaughtered, he received one shirt in his grave-bed. This brings great sorrow to every person at Dun-Sobhairce". The bards sang this sad saga through Dunseverick's halls to the accompaniment of an Irish harp.

In the year 795 the Vikings, Scandinavian adventurers, made their first incursion onto our north coast at Rathlin Island. We called them Ostmen. They stormed the castle in 870 and returned in 934.[9]

Then in 1177 the Normans reached this last bastion of the British islands. That fascinating English knight John de Courcy was created

Deirdre of The Sorrows. Oil. 20" x 20"

Governor of Ireland in 1185 after he had captured Downpatrick. In 1205 King John's[10] favour fell on Hugh de Lacy, who was created Earl of Ulster. Five years later, at Carrickfergus the King granted the lands of Dal Riata to Alanus de Galweia, the Earl of Athol. This patent was confirmed in 1215 and again in 1220.

The Normans built strong castles to display their power and erected fine churches to uphold their faith. Perhaps it was at that time that our fort removed from the Dun of Sobhairce to the defensible rock surrounded by the sea.[11] So it was in 1210 that Alanus erected the grand castle building. It was not as massive as Carrickfergus or Dundrum. The dressed basalt stones were closely fitted together by skilled masons. They used lime, gravel and sand to bind the mighty walls. The quoins were of beautifully cut basalt, a difficult achievement, which we Irish had never accomplished! The upper part of the rock is triangular in shape and rises a hundred feet above the sea. This was enclosed by a stout curtain wall. The entrance beyond the gorge was guarded by a defended gatehouse, some eighteen feet square. The bailey covered about three quarters of an acre in extent. The keep was thirty feet in length by twenty one feet in width. Beyond it lay a separate building for the kitchen and servants quarters. At the north-west corner, almost on the edge of the cliff there is the spring well. When I was a little boy, often I wondered how the sweet water remained therein.[12]

Not for long did the usurping English keep hold on this remote part of their united kingdom – *"In ultimis terrae"* as they called it. Then the O'Cahans came into their own.

When the Crusades were recruiting all the young bucks of Europe to claim back the Holy Land from the Infidels, Turlough O'Cahan made the long journey to Jerusalem to defend our religion.[13] He was absent from Dunseverick for several years. When he returned from the Holy Land he found that the Danes had occupied the castle in his absence.[14] Turlough's little sister had fallen in love with handsome Hakon Jarl, the youthful Danish leader. She agreed to accept Hakon's proposal of marriage on condition that the Dane became a good Christian. A monk from Cambus on the River Bann came swiftly to instruct the willing catechumen. Swiftly came the abbot of Bangor to baptise and tie the nuptial knot. Then Turlough appeared, fresh from the Crusades. *"Not with holy water will you be baptised but with Greek Fire"* From a vase he poured naphtha mixed with nitre and sulphur over Hakon Jarl. A violent death struggle ensued. Both men were incinerated. The castle blazed. The wedding guests jostled on the narrow causeway to escape. Turlough's sister, in flaming bridal garments, rushed to the edge of the cliff and hurled herself down the hundred feet drop into the sea of Moyle.

Often we heard the coronach of old Granie Roe, the O'Cahan banshee, howling on a winter's storm in a lament for Turlough, his sister, Hakon and what might have been had Danes and Irish been united in holy matrimony.

The years passed by and in 1565 Sean the Proud O'Neill captured Dunseverick castle and held it for a while. Sean was a boyo, or as we say in Irish *"A young gasoon"*. He took The O'Neillship for himself after murdering Conn O'Neill. He imprisoned and cuckolded his rival Calvach O'Donnell. Sean was one of the few men able to cozen Queen Elizabeth. Tongue in smiling cheek he swore allegiance and got all his demands by the Peace of Drumcree in 1563.[15] All life was his joke. He returned to the causeway coast and trounced the MacDonnells. That was when he captured our castle. Soon the Lord Deputy, Sir Henry Sidney removed the smile off Sean's handsome face. Then The O'Neill audaciously appealed to the MacDonnells for help! They remembered the cuckolding and gleefully murdered Sean on June 2, 1567. He was survived by a dozen landless and lawless larrikins who terrorised the countryside. Fortunately they left us alone in Dunseverick to enjoy a peaceful spell of life.

But not for long did the British allow us to settle our own little quarrels *"in ultimis terrae"*. The plantation of our country brought the English and the Scottish settlers in the early years of the seventeenth century. We Irish were driven from the good arable lands our fathers had tended from times immemorial. We had to take refuge in the Glens, the bogs and the wastelands.

During the winters of 1609 and 1610 hundreds of our local people died of starvation and exposure to the elements. Resentment was in the air. Prominent among the leaders of the Route were the O'Cahans. In May 1615, Rorie O'Cahan was beheaded for treason, a tragic day for the castle.

By 1641 the government could not restrain a revolution. The Irish from Derry crossed the River Bann, led by Turlough Oge O'Cahan and Allaster MacColl MacDonnell. They slaughtered thousands of British settlers. That was the second day of the new year 1642, ever afterwards it was known as Black Friday. To cut a long story short, General Munro came over from Scotland to restore order. In 1649 that black hearted villain, Cromwell, arrived to complete the job of subjugation.

It still pains me to recite the bloody vengeance that butcher vented on our people. Pure unadulterated vindictiveness earned Cromwell the hatred and contempt of the Irish people ever since.

Among the thousands that were massacred, were my father and my brother, beheaded at Carrickfergus Castle in 1653 – at I have told you. Then Cromwell's soldiers destroyed the castle. After 1657 it became a total ruin, as any house does when the roof falls and rains pours through the walls.

What was left of our people moved a few miles inland to where we had property at Ballinlea.[16]

Here we settled into the farming way of life. Around the winter hearth fires we recall our heros of olden days. Not many families can boast a heritage of five thousand years. In our own quiet way, we are very proud of our Irish story. Walk around the fishermen's path from Port Braddan and visit Dunseverick Castle.[17]

My ancestors will give you Cead Mile Failte.[18]

Finn builds the Causeway. Oil. 20" x 20".

AUTHOR'S NOTES

1. Oliver Cromwell embarked from Milford-Haven and landed at Ringsend near Dublin on August 14, 1649. His aim was to propagate the Commonwealth and the Gospel. This included the complete destruction of the Irish rebellion of 1641. He brought £200,000 (a vast sum of money in those days), six cavalry regiments, several troops of dragoons, an immense supply of bibles and thousands of scythes. The scythes were imported to bring in the August Irish harvest, as much to feed his forces as to deprive the Irish. The bibles were to convert the Catholic Irish to the Reformed Faith.

2. This was the Dun or Fort of Sobhairce (Dunseverick). Robert McCahan suggests it was a few hundred yards to the south of the present castle rock. Dunseverick was one of the three major forts in Ireland. Sobhairce was great-great grandson of Mil, the traditional ancestor of the Irish people. The Gaels, were the sons of Mil Espaine. Dunseverick castle is in the townland of *"Feigh Mountain"* Faiche means a green lawn.

3. Annus Mundi, the Year of the World. Annals of the Four Masters suggest the foundation date between B.C. 1692 and 1525.

4. The Tain Bo Cuailgne, in the Book of Leinster, records the story. The Queen of Connaught invaded Ulster to steal Donn Cuailgne (the famous-bull). She triumphed and before returning home burned the fort at Dunseverick. *"Maev fared north through Dalriada to ever-bright Dunseverick. She gave fierce battle and slew Findmore, the wife of Keltar. She pillaged all that famous dun and took fifty women as captives"*. Dunseverick was the landing place of Deirdre of the Sorrows and the sons of Usneach. (U.A.H.S.) (also see note 4 – "A letter from a Duchess".) Traditionally, after the crucifixion Joseph of Arimathea was imprisoned. When he was released by Emperor Vespasian in A.D. 63, he brought to Britain the holy grail and the spear by which Jesus was wounded. He founded Glastonbury Abbey.

5. Tripartite Life of Patrick.

6. Tara was a prehistoric complex associated with the seat of the high kings of Ireland, near Navan in County Meath. Five major roads radiated in straight lines from the hill. These were paved and had double lanes. Where they crossed bogland the roads were carried on oak timbers. The Slighe Miodhluachra was the main road to Donegal with branch routes to Armagh, Downpatrick and Dunseverick.

AUTHOR'S NOTES

7. There are two wells, one on the mainland near the Dun, which Robert McCahan suggests was the original site of the fort. The other well is a few feet from the north precipice, a hundred feet above sea level, yet it never becomes dry. Both are thought to be holy wells, whose water brings healing.

8. Armoy

9. *"The storming of Dun Sobhairce in Ulster"* (Irish Poem) claims this was the first time such an event had occurred (c870). The 924 or 934 attack was made by *"Danes from Lough Cuan" (Strangford).*

10. See my book "Holywood Then and Now" for the story of John de Courcy.

11. See Note (2) above.

12. See Note (7) above.

13. The crusades were undertaken by European Christians against Turks and Saracens for the recovery of the Holy Land and the honour of the Cross (Latin, crux.). 1st Crusade (1096-99) was initiated by Pope Urban II, captured Jerusalem for some years. 2nd (1147-49) was a failure. 3rd (1189-91) was led by Richard of England and Philip of France. Probably it was to this crusade Turlough O'Cahan gave his allegiance. 4th (1202-04) attacked Constantinople and attempted to found a Latin Empire. The Childrens' Crusade took place in 1212 – most perished or were sold into slavery. 5th (1228-29) secured Jerusalem for 15 years. 6th (1249) and 7th (1270) Crucades were unsuccessful.

14. A half mile from the castle is Benedanir Port with its fine basaltic columns. Haron Jarl may have landed here. Beinn an Danair means the Dane's peak or cliff.

15. Peace of Drumcree (1563). In 1562 Shane O'Neill (1530-1567) submitted to Elizabeth in London. The following year the Peace of Drumcree acceded to his demands for the O'Neillship. To show his loyalty to the crown, Shane attacked the MacDonnells and won a grand victory.

16. The people of Ballinlea met for Mass on Croaghmore mountain (cruach-a rick, a rick-like hill). After Penal times a chapel dedicated to St. Joseph, was erected. Today it is associated with the church at Ballintoy.

AUTHORS NOTES

17.   All that remains of Dunseverick Castle is the lower part of the square keep or tower. The property is in the safe keeping of the National Trust and is visited by thousands of tourists who walk "The Ulster Way" from the Giants Causeway to White Park Bay.

18.   A hundred thousand welcomes.

The sea of Moyle, between the Causeway Coast and Scotland, was the scene for two of the Sorrowful Stories of Ireland. The Children of Lir were changed into swans by their jealous step-mother for nine hundred years. They flew from Cashel to the north coast for safety. The ringing of the Margy Bell would change them back into children and bring peace to Ireland. Rosamund Praeger of Holywood, made this story the subject of a sculpture, which is in safe keeping by the National Trust, at the Causeway schoolhouse. The Praeger Bronze 'Girl asleep by fountain' accompanies the sculpture.

Deirdre of the Sorrows is the daughter of the king's storyteller and is the king's ward. The ageing king wishes to marry the beautiful young girl, but she has fallen in love with his nephew, Noisi. Deirdre, Noisi and his two brothers flee to Scotland to avoid the king's wrath. The king lures them home with falce promises. He takes Deirdre captive and slaughters the three boys. Deirdre dashes her brains against a rock rather than marry king Conchobar.

VIII THE SCHOOL MASTER'S LETTER

JOHN STURROCK, WHITE PARK BAY (1770 – 1777)

Greetings. Let me introduce myself to you, before I tell you something of the school which your Port Braddan Mill House overlooks.

I am not in any way an Irishman as you may tell from my name, William Sturrock, which the good folk of this north coast pronounce Sterick. My father was John Sturrock, a merchant of London city in England. I was inducted into the curacy of Culfeightrin parish on September 12, 1770. Along with Culfeightrin I was curate of Ballintoy from 1770 until the year 1777.

Seldom did I see my superior, the Rev. Dr. Edward Trotter, who had been Rector of Ballintoy since 1761. The good doctor was Prebendary of St. Andrews in the Cathedral of the Holy Trinity at Downpatrick, the locality of which is the rectory of Inch in the County Down, a long day's journey from Ballintoy! At that time there were only 450 families in the parish, so there was no great quantum of work for a mere curate. Dr. Trotter died on July 8, 1777 in London and was buried at St. James' Piccadilly. When the famous Rev. Robert Traill came to Ballintoy on August 19, 1777, my curacy terminated. Robert Traill was rector until 1842 – a ministry of sixty five years!

During my time at Ballintoy I conducted an educational establishment in the fine mansion house which John Stewart built in 1730 on the warrens and sand dunes of White Park Bay. I suppose, like myself, you have been confused by the multiplicity of leading Stewart families in the area. Let me explain the profundity of that prolific pedigree. The Ballintoy Castle family had retired to Action in County Armagh in 1760[1]. The Kilmahamogue Stewarts were residing at Drumtullagh and John Stewart owned the best positioned mansion on the Causeway Coast. Eventually the White Park family married with the Moores of Ballydivity and became the Stewart-Moores.

I shall take you on an informatory perambulation around our school campus which extends to one hundred and eighty acres. It must be finest adventure playground in Europe.

Your village, Port Braddan, divides of Causeway black basalt from the limestone of White Park Bay. The Port Braddan fault runs eastward straight over land from Runkerry and then under the sea to Ballintoy at a volcanic vent. The strand is a mile long extent of golden sands. The warren stretches to the south, once it was the sea beach. After the ice melted, the beach rose and the waves sculptured our majestic sand dunes.[2]

Our first ancestors arrived on White Park some nine thousand years ago, about the same time as the Mount Sandel settlement on the River Bann.[3] At that time sea level was lower than it is now. This allowed early man to make the coracle passage from Argyle into our deeply forested island. The white cliffs shining in the morning sunshine attracted the settlers from far out at sea. When they landed they were delighted to find precious flint nodules literally falling out of the chalk cliffs, which they had seen from their coracles.[4]

The hard nodules were like gifts from the gods, to our Mesolithic cousins. Soon carefully crafted tools, spears, scrapers and other weapons were being made from the crude lumps of flint. Exports from the White Park factory were sought all over the British Isles. Often I take my classes to the screes on

White Park House (reconstruction from extant foundations).

the south cliffs of White Park to search among rock debris for shaped chips of flint and rejected or unfinished articles. Some of the boys have very good collections of flint axe heads.

To the east of the school there is a tumulus or cairn atop a little hill, here was the special burial place of our early bronze age ancestors. Below the mound, in a broad hollow is a 'kitchen midden' or the Neolithic rubbish dump of early masons who worked the flint nodules.[5] The boys enjoy hunting through the fragmented debris in order to multiply their collections of flint implements.

Most days, during term time, I teach classes from eight of the clock till midday. That is each day except for the Sabbath, when the boys attend church-service. During the early evening we go on field trips or take recreation.[6] However, school time tables depend on the vagaries of the weather. We make full use of good sunny days for expeditions and stay indoors for study periods during times of rain and storm.

One of the field trips which my students most enjoy is the excursion to the caves. There are many caves in the area. Most are natural caverns in the coastal cliffs but there are many on the farms of Ballintoy parish. In England and France we designate the latter as souterrains; in Ireland they are called caves! In fact they are artificially constructed tunnels, close to a rath in which to take refuge in times of danger. Today they are used as hiding places and often disclose interesting antique items. In Ireland raths are often called forts. They are the remains of enclosed farm steads, where circular ramparts of earth and surrounding ditches were constructed for safety. Above the White Park cliffs we have three megaliths or dolmens, which we explore during history lessons. The local people call these Druids altars! In fact they indicate the position of an important tomb and consist of a large flat slab supported on two or more vertical stones. The name comes from the Cornish word *"Tolmen"* – a hole (in a) stone, from the aperture formed by the slabs.

The most interesting of the shoreline caverns are the four caves which delve into the high cliffs between Carrick-a-Raide[7] and Kenbane Castle.[8] On a good day, when the sea is calm, (a essential fact) we take our trumpets and an appetizing school picnic and proceed to Ballintoy Harbour. There we hire three or four boats for the exciting voyage to the formidable Carrick-a-Raide. Soon we are navigating the narrow chasm between the two hundred feet perpendicular cliffs. All is excitement!

Three of the adjoining caves extend for considerable lengths into the cliffs. The fourth is short but has a magnificent sixty foot Gothic arch entrance. We row into each of the caves and blow on our trumpets. The echoes re-sound again and again through each of the caves at different keys. They produce one harmonic cord. The symphonic poem expertly performed is inexpressibly beautiful. If one had sufficient trumpeters, a full orchestral performance could be achieved. I must confess this is my only music lesson for my young students!

After a sea-board picnic we always visit Buillacoocullian. This fissure, only three feet wide, rises forty feet through smooth white limestone. Of course, the bards among us recite the story of Cuchulainn's magic sword that made the cavernous cut in solid rock. Now we commence the return passage to Ballintoy, our flailing oars avoiding ominous Craigmananan, the submarine rocks hidden by the waves, where Mananan, Ireland's greatest magician threw himself into the sea of Moyle![9]

Now let me tell you of another cave which our White Park seminary students often visit. They call it the Englishman's cave. I know not who this Sassenach was, but his cave is situated at the east end of the bay. I understand he erected a stone and lime wall across the high entrance and build therein a stout front door. Inside his dark palace he had three natural rock rooms. The largest is some forty five by fifteen feet with a ceiling nine feet in height.

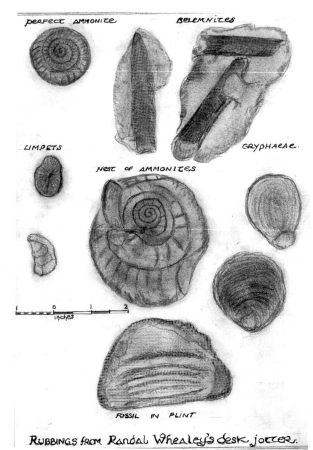

PERFECT AMMONITE   BELEMNITES   LIMPETS   GRYPHAEAE. NEST OF AMMONITES   FOSSIL IN FLINT

RUBBINGS FROM Randal Whealey's desk jotter.

A smaller room provided him with a snug little bed chamber. Above there is a third cave, in the form of an attic room, which is approached by a narrow passage. In fact, it is a better dwelling than many of the single room cottages in the parish.

When the Englishman departed, (for what reason I know not) a few local lads realised the remote situation provided an excellent site for an illicit distillery. Poteen was produced by the bucketful, along the lines of the Bushmills distillery which was founded in 1608.[10]

The poteen business prospered and developed into a smuggling concern, using the local harbours for transportation of contraband liquor. The privateers even acquired a small cannon to keep off uninvited visitors! The Englishman's attic room was particularly useful in which to still the poteen. Nowadays the caves are used as a potato store, but our boys are intrigued by the licentious history.

Resulting from the great number of birds on White Park Bay, ornithology has been a study subject since the school was established. The selection of species is quite amazing. Let me catalogue a few, in case you would like to make a tally. Our boys compile registers with dates of ornithological sightings. These they leave behind for future school generations when their school days are over.

We have recorded the following birds: ravens, jackdaws, gannets, blackbirds, chaffinch, turnstone, little wrens, oyster catchers, thrush, sky larks, robins, pipits, fulmar petrels and herring gulls. Cormorants, razorbills, guillemots, kittiwares, elder ducks, chough, rock doves, peregrine falcons, buzzards and even grouse and pheasants which have saved their lives by lucky escape from the local estates!

Imagine our excitement on the first day of last summer term, when young Robert Stewart saw a great alk. None of us had ever seek an alk at White Park, although we had found alk bones in the 'kitchen mittens'. It is a cousin of the razorbill and guillemot but is incapable of flight as its wings are not fully developed – rather like those of penguins. All the boys are keeping their eyes skinned, in case our great alk pays us a second visit before the end of term and the long vacation commences.

Some of my boys are more interested in fossils than feathered friends! At the Port Braddan end of White Park Bay, nearest to your mill, the white chalk cliff gives up many fossils. The word comes from Latin "fossilis" 'dug up' (from fodere, to dig). It seems originally it denoted a fossilised fish which was thought to have lived underground!

At the west end of the bay, the hard hitting hand hammers of our fossil hunters oust ammonites and belemnites from the soft chalk cliff face. Ammonites are extinct sea animals or mollusc. They were protected within a partitioned spiral shell which became fossilised in the chalk. When they were classified, recently in this century, etymologists gave them the Latin title *'Cornu Ammonis' – 'The Horn of Ammon.'* The beautiful little objects resemble a ram's horn which characterises representations of the Egyptian god Ammon.

Belemnites are the fossilised cylinder–shaped internal shells of an extinct order of cephalopods of the Mesozoic period. Recent cataloguers have given them the tag belemnite, from the Greek *'Dart'*. Usually the seeker will discover only the circular cross-section of the fossil.

Our best fossil finding field trip was the day last year when one of the Whealey boys let a flint nodule fall on his foot! As usual he had been throwing stones at his peers, entirely against my instructions. So we all laughed profusely while Whealey yelled to high heaven. Suddenly his lamentations ceased. The nodule had split open to reveal a huge cluster of violet coloured agates, which positively scintillated in the morning sunshine. These are a hard fine-grained form of chalcedony or translucent quartz. In it microscopic crystals are packed together in parallel bands. It is rather like the columnar basalt of the Giant's

Causeway pillars. In fact the causeway columns are the big brothers of these tiny sisters of White Park Bay. The name comes from a Greek word meaning *"A mystical stone,"* Chalcedon, an ancient city on the Bosporus. Agate, also Greek, comes from the name of a river in Sicily.

There was much envy when young Whealey carried his great cluster of amethysts into the dormitory. He asked me the meaning of the word; it was the first time the wretched boy had ever shown any interest in the classics! I told him it comes from the Greek word *'Amethustos' – 'not intoxicating.'*. This derives from the unfortunate belief that amethyst prevents drunkenness! I understand the mystical stone enclosing the great cluster of amethysts is in safe keeping at your mill house. From the above lesson you can see how we combine the essential study of classics with the physical sciences of which White Park Bay is a spectacular outdoors laboratory. It is covered with specimens awaiting experiment.

One experiment I do not encourage is the well known White Park mud game. In history classes, the boys learn that the Ballintoy ladies of the Neolithic age smeared yellow ochre over their bodies in order to improve the work of nature. Our boys emulate the beauty aid by clobbering one another with great lumps of ochre. Strangely it is the one Greek word they all remember – Okhros – 'pale yellow'. They chant *'Okhros Okhros'* as they hurl handfuls of White Park ochre at each other. The game has become quite a school tradition, I am sorry to tell you!

I shall spare you the stories of our green sand, the lignite and bauxite mines, the oyster-like gryphaeae fossils and the malleable blue clay from which we made our excellent tennis court.

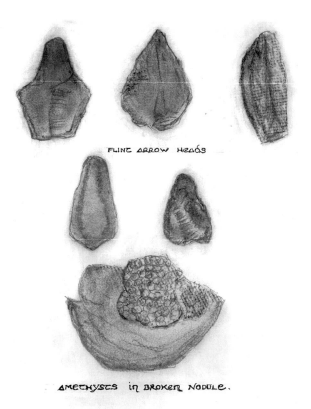

FLINT ARROW HEADS

AMETHYSTS IN BROKEN NODULE.

Rubbings from Randal Whealey's desk jotter.

However, the school's Ball Alley was soundly constructed on deep foundations down by the little stream which skirts the mansion house. The special open air court keeps the students out of mischief, all the year round. Some of them are remarkably proficient at the popular game of Ball. I wish there were other schools in the area with which we should be able to compete in field sports. Alas, Foyle College in Londonderry and the Belfast Academy are our nearest neighbours!

The local fauna seems to welcome the addition

of the Ball Alley. Birds nests in it and foxes make lairs beneath the floor. Their distinctive odour assails the nostrils when one goes down to play ball. Often I see the little foxes chasing each other over the sand dunes on bright moonlit nights. Along with the foxes our fauna includes Irish hares who box together, rabbits galore, shy badgers, a breed of edible snails, and several species of rare insects. We have a living show-case for nature-study, a most important subject on our curriculum.

Among my students are not a few notability, also many a scholar, although I say it myself. Of local families the Ballintoy Stewarts and their many cousins, the Whealeys and the Bushmills Macnaghtens received their early education here. Robert Stewart, who became the Viscount Castlereagh, and second Marquis of Londonderry (1769 to 1822) benefited from my tutelage. He entered the Royal School at Armagh in 1780 and St. John's College, Cambridge some six years later. In 1790 Robert became a member of the Irish House of Commons, representing the County Down, as the family live at Mountstewart on the Ards Peninsula.[11]

Lord Castlereagh carried through the Act of Union (1800) incorporating Ireland within the United Kingdom. This he did in the hope that Catholic emancipation would ensue. As Chief Secretary, he successfully fought a duel with the Foreign Secretary; organised the alliance which overthrew Napoleon and master-minded the sequential congress which brought peace to Europe (1815). Not a bad record for a young lad who ran on the sands and swam in the cold water of White Park Bay! Sorry to say he committed suicide on August 12, 1822; but we can not be held responsible for that sad event.

A couple of the Macnaghten boys gained influence far beyond the ambit of our little school. Edward became Lord of the Treasury and Francis was the Chief Justice of Calcutta in India.

I hope I have painted an interesting picture of our White Park Bay seminary. I am sorry I must now move onward to pastures new. The young Rev. Robert Traill has been appointed Rector of the Parish. I wish him and the school all prosperity.[12]

Horas non numero nisi serenas.[13]

Robert Stewart and Francis Macnaghten in the Seminary Ball Alley.

75

AUTHOR'S NOTES

The installation of Rev. Robert Traill took place at Ballintoy in 1777. Rev. William Sturrock left the parish and presumably the seminary. I am unable to discover if the school continued after his retirement. Ordance Survey memoirs record White Park House was build about 1735. By 1838 a portion of the dwelling was used by the waterguard officer but the other improvements had fallen to decay. During the 20th Century it became a youth hostel and then a week-end cottage on the farm of Mr Dan Logan. The property was acquired by the National Trust which turned the remains of White Park House into a public toilet. The facility was vandalised shortly afterwards.

1.   See 'A letter from the last Stewart'.

2.   The most recent ice age occurred during the Pleistocene epoch, about 12,000 years ago. It determined the total amount of sand on White Park Bay. Amounts removed for agricultural and domestic purposes can not be replaced by nature.

3.   Mountsandel Fort was first fortified in the Iron Age and continued in use until the 17th century. The site provides outstanding information about the Mesolithic Age and Ireland's first inhabitants.

4.   A coracle is a small round boat made from animal skins stretched over a wicker frame. In Ireland, it is called a currach from (Gaelic) *'Curach'* which means a small boat.

5.   Nodules are roundish lumps found in the chalk when the silica has segregated from its calcareous matrix. Where they are found in quantity, commercial mining of chalk is difficult as they blunt the machinery. They were invaluable to the flint workers.

6.   It is interesting to note at this time the word *'afternoon'* was not in common usage. The day was divided into night, morning, noonday and evening. Sites visited to the south of Whitepark Bay were Cloghabogil, the two cromlechs, the bauxite mines Dunboy, Castlelea, Dunshammer and Dundrif, the artificially flattened motte at the east end of the bay.

7.   Carrick A Raide – the rock in the road. Today the 25 meter sea chasm is bridged by the famous rope bridge during the summer season. Formerly a fishing industry operated from the rock, which was in the road of salmon, swimming towards the river Bush. A second meaning is *"Rock of the throwing"*. Sheep island, an important bird sanctuary, is offshore.

AUTHOR'S NOTES

8.   Kenbane Castle (White Headland) was built in 1547 by Colla MacDonnell. It was taken by the English in 1551 but restored for habitation by the MacDonnells. Grace Staples' cave cuts through the promontory.

9.   Ordance Survey memories of August 1830 (recorded by Lieutenant Thomas Hore) claim:

    (a) "The Giant, Cut', the Bridge and the Causeway are among the great natural curiosities frequently visited by strangers to the area".

    (b) Craig Mananan is an enchanted rock, dangerous to all mariners on the north coast. Mananan, who drowned himself here, was an extraordinary magician. After death he continued to prosecute his magic on the rock".

10.   Bushmills claims to have the world's oldest distillery. In 1276 English forces campaigning in north Antrim were given "a mighty draft of usquebaugh (water of life) before battle ". In 1608 James I granted a license to distil whiskey. Four years later the Lord Mayor of London (William Cockayne) had to sell property to pay for his imports of Bushmills whiskey. In 1697 the Czar of Russia (Peter The Great) considered Irish whiskey the best of all beverages.

11.   This branch of the Stewart family initially received land in Co. Donegal during the Plantation of Ulster (c. 1609). Robert Stewart (1739-1821) purchased the Co. Down estate in 1744. He became a Baron in 1789 and Marquis of Londonderry in 1816. His son was a student at the White Park Bay Seminary.

12.   This would have taken place in the summer of 1779.

13.   "I count only the sunny hours". (A school master should remember only the happy times).

IX A LETTER FROM THE LAST STEWART.

ALEXANDER STEWART, BALLINTOY (1750 – 1790)

Around Dublin City and in County Armagh they call me "Graceless Alex"[1] – after my father. He did not deserve such an inelegant epithet, as he lived the polished life of a country gentleman and did much good in his day! Of myself, I can say I emulated his example only in a dedicated ability to get rid of money as quickly as possible. My clever old grandmother wrote a humorous piece about my father under that ridiculous name Roderick Random. Concerning myself she could only say I would bring the family to an ignominious end, thus I never lived down that graceless synonym.

Let me tell you about our family – the Stewarts of Ballintoy. I know you can see the tower of our church from the windows of your mill house at Port Braddan. Once you would have been able to see the spire, however it flew away like most of our property. You can still tell the time of day by the sundial on the tower's south side and the height of the tides at Ballintoy harbour by the moon dial.

In the first decade of the sixth Christian century three Stewart brothers Loarn, Angus and Fergus joined the Scottes in an expansion into Argyle from Dal Riata on the Antrim Coast.

In those far off days, Erin and Isla became linked by more than blood or water. During the atrocious winters of 684 and 695 cousins could visit over a bridge of glass. The channel was frozen between the islands. Over the succeeding years, a close contact was kept between Scotland and Ireland.[2]

To look at me, "Graceless Alec" you would not think that from the Stewarts of Ballintoy sprang Dal Riatic kings, including Robert Bruce, the victor of Bannockburn and from him the Scottish monarchy. Foolishly, our branch of the family joined in an unsuccessful rebellion instigated by King Henry VIII, during the minority of Mary. Of course, we lost some of our lands in Argyle, Bute and Arran.

So in the middle of the sixteenth century, new lands were required and a return to the Route and the Causeway Coast seemed the logical solution to our financial difficulties.[3]

During the year 1625 Randal MacDonnell, 1st Earl of Antrim, granted Ballylough and Ballintoy to Archibald Stewart, with "Sheep Island and the other little islands of the Camplie," thrown into the deal for good luck. In April of that year John Macnaghten, his Lordship's agent, legally completed the grant, at an annual rent of nine pounds stirling. When Macnaghten died Stewart was appointed land agent to Lord Antrim.

The second Lord Antrim succeeded to the earldom in 1636. He was a different kettle of fish to his congenial father. I understand you have description of the gentleman from his lady wife, in the collection of letters to your Port Braddan mill. So you will know what I mean when I say His Lordship was rather demanding.[4]

During the terrible times of the Irish Rebellion in 1641, the irresponsible Lord Antrim preferred the safety of the Dublin Pale, to the wilds of the North. My ancestor, Alexander Stewart, had to hold together the Causeway Coast estates for the Antrim family, although he never claimed to be much of a fighting man! Later the boastful Earl fell foul of King Charles I and again left his agent to carry the can. The difficulties of the times took their course, as they always do, and things came back to normal.

Here I should give you a short note on the abundant proliferation of the Stewarts in North Antrim. The first James Stewart settled in the Route about 1560. His family included Archibald, Minian, David, Jane and Christian. Lord Antrim's agent, Archibald married Jane McCullough by whom he left a dozen procreative Stewarts – William, George, Robert, Alexander, Lewis, Christian, Isabella, Mary, Grizzel, Jane, Alice and little Rose!

You will be amused to know the names of your neighbours around Port Braddan and the Route, who can claim descent from the vast Ballintoy family. McConaghys, McCurdys, McCoys, McAllisters, McNeills, McMullins, McMullans, McAulays, McLaughlins, McCaws, McCambridges, McIlattons, McKeemanus, McKeevers Boyds, Blacks, Browns, Cusacks, Hutchinsons, Fullertons, Hamills, Hills, Kanes, Lynns, Loughreys, Magees, Orrs, Ramsays, Rogers, Sinclairs, Scallys Steeles and Wallaces – in fact most of the country side!

My illustrious ancestor, land agent Archibald Stewart, became a member of the Irish House of commons. In 1662 a serious dispute arose between Stewart and Dr. Ralph King, a fellow Irish parliamentarian.[5] It seems the doctor had been collecting rents in the Barony of Carey and Rathlin Island. Alexander declared the money should have been swelling the Stewart coffers and procured an order from the House of Lords to prevent Doctor King's agent collecting the disputed rents.

The Commons took umbrage that one of its members would take a dispute with a fellow member to the House of Lords for settlement. The members thought that dirty linen should not be washed in public. All this occurred in May 1662. On the following June 3rd Stewart recanted. It seems Archibald learned nothing from the fracas. On February 10,1665 again he recanted in a similar accusation, which he had made against Peter Beagham, Esq., M.P.

Of the parliamentary Stewarts only one daughter – Bernarda – lived to inherit the family properties. She married her cousin James Stewart of the Straid, in 1650. Bernarda died in 1663 and was entombed under the chancel of Ballintoy Church. The following year James inherited the few remaining estates of Ninian Stewart in Bute. It seems James sold the properties as soon as they came into his possession.

Ballylough House.

The family had no intention of returning to Scotland. Four years later, on September 10, 1667, James and Bernarda's little son Nicholas died. He was buried beside his mother in Ballintoy Church.[6]

A sister of Nicholas, named Mary, married Richard Dobbs of Dobbs Castle, Carrickfergus. This was an extremely fortunate union. Their son Arthur became the first brain-box our family produced. Arthur's consummate passion was to discover a new sea passage to India. In 1744 his essay on the subject encouraged the British government to dispatch a couple of ships to explore the possible existence of the North West Passage. His other publications were "An Account of Captain Middleton's Voyage to Hudson's Bay" and 'Trade of Ireland'. In 1753 he was appointed Governor of North Carolina. This was promotion indeed for a boy from Ballintoy!

Bernarda's sister Alice, married a Scottish soldier who had been serving in the Ulster army of Charles I. Major Alexander MacAuley and Alice went around the coast to live at Glenville, Cushendall. Their grandson Dr. Alexander MacAuley became Judge of the Consistoral Court in Dublin. He died in 1766.

Sara, youngest sister of Alice and Bernarda presented the communion chalice and paten to Ballintoy Church in 1684. About the same time their brother Charles had the church bell re-cast. I suppose some sort of refurbishment of our ecclesiastical property was going on at that time.

Brother Charles married a daughter of Sir Toby Poyntz. This propitious union added five thousand acres of prime Irish pasture to the family coffers. The lands are the Acton estate at Pontzpass in the County Armagh. Charles was a colonel in the army of King William and was very active in the military organisation of the Province. Our family tradition

Ballyloogh gatelodge.

says he went to London about 1688 and died there in 1710. Colonel Charles Stewart and his wife had two sons Archibald and Alexander. They also had a daughter called Jane, my great aunt.

An amusing family story is told of my great aunt Jane. Apparently she was a progressive thinker and had firm beliefs on the proper education of the local children around Ballintoy. She bequeathed fifteen pounds per annum to employ a suitable school master in the village. Usually such benefactions were in the gift of the local rector. Aunt Jane thought otherwise. She determined that the appointment of the school-master should be made by the parents of the children, they were the parishioners of Ballintoy meeting at the Easter Vestry. This democratic direction brought considerable difficulties to our peaceful village.[7]

Jane's elder brother was the Rev. Doctor Archibald Stewart, Chancellor of Connor. He was born at Acton in 1677 became a graduate of Trinity College Dublin in 1700 and received his doctorate in 1722. In 1714 he married Leonora Vesey, daughter of the Bishop of Tuam. Their only child died accidentally, shortly after birth. The baby arrived twenty years after the couple were married. On this account the parents thought their infant son was a physically delicate child. They used the usual eighteenth century remedy to improve poor constitution. Daily the unfortunate child was dipped into cold water for his morning bath in the nursery at Ballintoy Castle. On the morning of the tragedy the baby was plunged rapidly on three occasions. The poor child did not get time to recover breath and so failed to survive the cure! As you may suppose there was great grief among the Castle family and in the town of the north. Having been given one child so late in life, Archibald and Leonora remained childless.

Rev. Archibald Stewart served as army Chaplin to Queen Anne during the war of the Spanish Succession (1702-1713).[8] He inherited the Ballintoy and Acton estates in 1710 and resided at Ballintoy Castle, when he returned from the continental wars. In 1718 he became Rector of Ballintoy and Billy, which cures he held until 1737 when he was promoted to the Chancellorship of Connor. It seems about this time a removal from Ballintoy Castle to Ballylough occurred; The Chancellor died at Ballylough on May 13, 1760.

Dr. Stewart's younger brother inherited the estates. In the early years of the eighteenth century Archibald and Alexander of Action (and by chance Ballintoy) were the most eligible young gentlemen in the Province.

About 1720 Alexander was appointed Agent to the Earl of Antrim, who was a minor. The position had been in the gift of Lord and Lady Massereene, the Earl's legal guardians. They found Alexander Stewart a satisfactory and faithful agent; their ward thought otherwise!

Shortly after Lord Antrim gained his majority (1734) he realised his lavish lifestyle was impoverishing the estate. Land sales were required to balance the annual expenditure. Perhaps it was guile which made the Earl accuse his agent of *"conniving low price sales to secure his own advantage and selfish purposes"*. The celebrated lawsuits which ensued, spread leisurely and expensively over the years 1740 and 1741. Alexander Stewart was completely exonerated of cupidity. The costs severely depleted the coffers of the Massereene estate.

Lord Antrim's agent, Alexander Stewart, was my grandfather. He married his cousin Anne, who was the daughter of John Stewart of Jamaica. My grandmother Anne, brought a very large dowry to the union. She produced two daughters and one son – Alexander T. Stewart, my father.

As ever, increase in family wealth was paralleled only by our extravagance! It was this ostentation that earned my father the local title *'Graceless Alex'*. His mother Anne, *"a lady highly accomplished and remarkably endowed by nature"* wrote a piece about her son Alexander under the nickname of the time *"Roderick Random"*[9] This very adequately described my fathers character and habits. He married a sister of Sir Hugh Hill of Derry, who was my dear mother.

You must not think my prodigal pater was completely useless. In 1757 he attempted to develop the economic advantages of the Ballintoy estate. The Irish House of Commons was successfully petitioned for grants to develop the Ballintoy coal mines. Claims were substantiated that *"Great quantities of coals had been exported to Dublin and other parts of the kingdom"*. The Stewarts were never known to underrate a good story!

Of course, the export of coal required a good

harbour, so Alexander spent £500 of his own money, to construct the new Ballintoy quay. He obtained a government grant of £2000 to complete the work, claiming Ballintoy was the only safe harbour between Larne and Derry. Financially the harbour was as thirsty as the sea which it served!

In 1759 the entrepreneurial Alexander came back, cap in hand to the Irish parliament for an additional £1,123 to complete the coal quay construction works.

The following year my father's pecuniary ventures came to an abrupt end. We were forced to sell up the Ballintoy property.

The estate was sold in Belfast to a Mr Cupples for £20,000. The castle and the townlands fell from our family's grasp. We came to reside permanently to our Acton estates in County Armagh. Soon afterwards my father paid the supreme sacrifice for his overindulgent lifestyle.

I have studied hard to live up to my father's graceless name and jocundity. I spend most of my time in Dublin's high society. My friends and co-Hedonists are the notorious Messrs. Whaley and Maguire. Last evening, at the club, we were highly amused when Whaley accepted our bets to jump out of a second-storey window onto the Dublin mail coach, which happened to be passing at full speed!

Indubitably it is unwise to get on the wrong side of my crony Maguire. He can trim a candlewick with a single pistol ball without extinguishing the flame, so great is his expertise as a duellist. When Maguire shouts *"jump"* I always levitate as high as my portly presence will allow!

In closing, let me tell you I have lived life to the full, and all my family property is mortgaged to the hilt. I never seemed to find time to get a wife or produce an heir. This is just as well as there is nothing to inherit! I am the last of the main line of the Ballintoy Stewarts.

Avito Viret Honore.[10]

Ballylough gates.

AUTHORS NOTES

Alexander Stewart died in 1790. With his death the male line of the Ballintoy branch of the family came to an end. In 1760 Alexander T. Stewart sold Ballintoy Castle to Mr Cupples of Belfast. Shortly afterwards Cupples sold it to Dr. Alexander Fullerton. On each occasion the sale price was £20,000. Dr. Fullerton had returned recently from the West Indies with a considerable fortune.

Originally the Fullertons were a Norwegian family who had settled on the Causeway Coast at the same time as the Stewarts. William Fullerton assisted Alexander Stewart to hold Ballintoy Castle against the Irish insurgents in 1641.

Dr. Alexander Fullerton bequeathed the property to his niece, the wife of Dawson Downing of Bellaghy, whose son took the name Downing Fullerton. Her grandson, Alexander George, married Lady Georgina Leverson Gower, daughter of Lord Granville. (Later family connection with Northern Ireland is noted). The estate remains in the ownership of the Downing-Fullertons.

The Dowings gave their name to the Downing Street property in London where the Prime Minister's house and other Government buildings were erected. The choice of the Whitehall property or an estate in East Anglia was given to Downing College, Cambridge University when Sir George Downing founded that educational institution. East Anglia was chosen!

Ballintoy Castle was demolished in 1795. The grand oak staircase, fine panelling and valuable house beams were acquired from the sale to embellish Downing College.

Ballintoy Castle, County Antrim
AUCTION SALE
MONDAY, 10th DAY OF AUGUST, 1795

The material of the Castle recently taken down. Various scantings of old oak from eighteen feet long and nine inches square, downward. Slates of excellent size and quantity. Windows, Doors, etc., etc. The Sale will begin at ten o'clock. Lots will be made agreeable to bidders, 28th July, 1795.

Ballintoy Castle occupied the site known as 'The Castle' today. It is a half mile to the west of the village and about a quarter mile from the sea. The McShane family meticulously care for the modern buildings on the site.

The ancient castle must have been a mansion house of considerable size. The Hearth Money Rolls for 1669 claim it contained twelve hearths. Ordnance Memoirs (Lieutenant Thomas Hore,) 6 April 1838 writes.

"Of this once splendid and extensive building, nothing now remains but 65 feet in length of the rear wall of one of the squares. It varies from 2 to 10 feet high, 2 and a half feet thick, corners of cut free stone

and the remainder of whin quarry stone, and bound together by grouted mortar similar to other ancient buildings. Several of the office houses, garden walls, court walls are still extant, but much disfigured by dilapidation and sundry alterations. There was a handsome fish-pond, together with the grounds surrounding it, enclosed by a high stone and lime wall. The castle, towers, court yards, gardens, yards and other enclosures were very extensive, as may be seen by the ruins now extant, and all walls and parapets of stone and lime and strongly built of best materials. The office houses are changed to dwelling and office houses to accommodate farmers who at present reside on the site and farm the demesne. The castle was pulled down abut 40 years back by the present proprietor Fullerton Downing Esq. And the timber and other valuable materials sold by auction".

1. The Acton Demesne was founded by the Poyntz family of Iron Acton, Gloucestershire, in the eighteen century.

2. "I can go over on a bridge of glass. I can come over on a bridge of glass. If the glass bridge break there's none in Isla nor Eirinn who can mend the bridge of glass". (Chronicon Scotorum A.D. 684 and 695)

3. The Stewarts were descended from Sir John Stewart of Bute. About 1560 Sir John's sons escaped to Dunseverick, settled at Ballinstraid, then Ballintoy.

4. To read the alternative opinion see *"The Letter of the Duchess of Buckingham"*.

5. The return of Charles II to the throne of Ireland brought the Restoration parliament to Dublin (1661 to 1666). Alexander Stewart was an M.P. The first Irish parliament dated back to the thirteenth century. The Irish Lords first met as a separate House in the fourteenth century.

6. A red free stone slab under the holy table records: *"Under this stone Bernarda Stewart doth lie, who pangful death overcame victoriously 1663".*

    Nearby another stone is inscribed.
    "Here lies Nicholas Stewart who departed this life 10th of September 1667. When tender plants such as this childe by nature comely, courteous, mild, have Christian like outrun their race not earth but heaven have for their place, let us behind implore His grace that quickly we may see His face."

AUTHOR'S NOTES

7.   A reference to this arrangement is made in *'The Rector's Letter'*.

8.   The European States wished to prevent a Franco-Spanish monarchy in Spain and supported the claims of Austria. Marlborough gained control for Britain. (It was during this war that Gibraltar was captured from Spain).

9.   *"The Adventures of Roderick Random"* (1748) a novel by Tobias Smollett. The young Scottish scapegrace in quest of fortune, narrates a succession of dissolute and preposterous adventures. Eventually he redeems the family fortunes and scorns those relatives who rejected him.

10.   The Stewart Family moto *"He flourishes with ancestral honour"*.

. On campus, Downing College, Cambridge U.e.

X A LETTER FROM A UNITED IRISHMAN

JOHN CURRY. TONDUFF, 1770-1830

My name is John Curry. I work the family farm at Tonduff, about an Irish mile to the south of the Causeway's Benbane Head and our lovely Tonduff mountain. The village lies between the Aird with its Orange Hall and Carrowreagh with its Masonic Lodge.

Dunseverick Castle, fronting its Feigh, is further along the road. Many the times I passed it on my way down to Port Braddan and Gid Point for the fishing in the summer time.

Well I known the kindly family who live down at Braddan. Of course, they fish the salmon, we have to content ourselves with the glashen and rock codling, which at times you can pull out of the sea by the bucketful.

There are a couple of hundred acres of marsh and moss in Lisserliss and Tonduff mountain but in Tonduff townland there are two hundred acres of Antrim's fine arable soil. Our family came over from the Isles, towards the end of the sixteenth century. We managed to hold unto our land during those terrible years of rebellion, which became the cradle in which the carnage of Cromwell was conceived.[1]

When the Prince of Orange, William III, was declared our sovereign, after the revolution of 1688, my family gave him our full allegiance. The Irish supported the old king, James II, who fled to Ireland after that glorious revolution, seeking support to regain his crown. Three of our family were in Derry when the Jacobites besieged the Maiden City.[2] The massive stone walls defended the town. Apprentice boys slammed the gates shut in Lord Antrim's face and the citizens withstood one hundred and five days of siege. The Tonduff menfolk had to devour rat, cat and dog flesh, fattened on fifteen thousand corpses. When the Jacobites abandoned Williamite supporters under the walls, the defenders threatened to hang their Jacobite prisoners. Those were terrible days indeed!

At last the boom on the River Foyle was broken on July the 28th and British ships, laden with fresh food, effectively ended the seige.[3] My relatives came home to Tonduff, diseased and starving. The following year King Billy himself came to Ireland and defeated the Jacobite army of French and Irish in the battle across the River Boyne, which event we celebrate annually to this day.

I was born in the year 1770 at Tonduff and grew up on our farm with a deep affection for dogs and horses and cattle. In 1794 I met a lovely Scottish lassie called Lizzie MacLeod who hailed from the Isle of Skye. She was visiting a neighbouring family in Lisnagunogue. Lizzie was attending one of our local hoolies.[4] As soon as I set my eyes on her, I knew she must become my wife. She thought the same way as I did and the following springtime I went over to Skye to claim her as my bride. There was great joy and celebration when our first child arrived in 1796. We call him John, as all the first born of the Curry family.

Now I was a family man I resolved to make provision for a good well-heeled home. Towards this purpose I started to attend the cattle fairs at Ballycastle and Ballymoney. Soon I was known around the Causeway Coast as Honest John, whose hand spit sealed a square deal.[5]

I was building up a prosperous business when the year 1798 burst upon us with modern ferocity. Ballymoney has always been a free-thinking town and many of the young gassons around the cattle market were fired with the desire for the freedom of the times. Many a time my wife Lizzie chided me when I returned late to Tonduff on a market day. The only excuse I could offer my dear one was that we had been talking *"politics"* long into the night in the local ale-house. Of course, she could not understand such a waste of time.

In the years gone past many Bushmills families had left the Causeway Coast for the American colonies. After 1789 many wrote home praising the freedom of the new United States of America. In *'The Northern Star'* the newspaper to which thousands subscribed after 1792, we followed the revolution in France stroke by stroke. In Ballymoney we started to believe that a little bit of civil, political and religious liberty might not go amiss!

So it was that the boys sent up to Belfast to discover how to set up a local branch of the Society of United Irishmen. With many a laugh we all took the Oath.[6]

When the time came we were all too willing to support the half million who thought the way we did, in those long fourteen days of insurrection. Of course, the government saw us as a secret oath-bound brotherhood, thirsting for armed revolution.

On the eight of June our leader, Henry Joy McCracken, commanded four thousand volunteers in the battle of Antrim.[7] My Ballymoney friends were there to a man. At first the battle was a grand success for us. I saw Lord O'Neill fall head long from his horse, when one of our boys hacked through his splendid uniform with a bloody pike. Then additional government forces arrived on the scene and we were put to flight. Henry Joy McCracken was captured and executed.

Then came to aid my training for running and rowing races at White Park Bay and the long nights I had spent hunting on the Croagh Mountain.[8] I sprinted down the back lanes of Antrim Town to the Six Mile Water and almost succeeded in gaining the Lough Neagh shore. A posse attempted to arrest me. I slew each one of them with my pike, jumped into the river and escaped.

Under cover of darkness I got home to Tonduff. Lizzie, disapproving and tight lipped silent, patched up my many wounds. However, I dared not stay in our farm house, for the soldiers would come in the

Croaghmore Church.

morning, searching for this outlaw. For outlaw I was, John Curry, with five hundred pounds stirling on his head – dead or alive!

Over on the Feigh mountain behind our house there is an old cave, where we used to play when we were children. This damp cavern became my cell for two long months, as I lay recuperating from my wounds. Every night Lizzy sent my wee dog Barny to the cave with a bag of food tied to his collar. Oh, but it was good to see the wee article and feel his hot licks on my swollen hands and face.

One night there was a letter from Lizzie in the bag. A sheep had fallen into a deep gully. My wife did not have the strength to deal with the situation. It was August, so first light was about four of the clock. I ventured out to save my sheep.

That was my downfall. A runner-in from Coleraine, who recently had rented a neighbouring farm, saw me in the lane. He hastened to Ballycastle to inform the army captain and claim the five hundred pounds bounty money.

The soldiers searched our house and yard every day and night for a week, but did not suspect my hide-out. Then one night Lizzie sent a message with my dog Barny, that our little boy Johnny was very ill. Of course, I went down to the farmhouse as soon as possible.

No sooner was I through our back door than a detachment of soldiers was seen on the Causeway Road. The previous day Lizzie, my cautious dear, had hollowed out a hiding place in the middle of a stack in our yard. Into it I crept and Lizzie replaced the sheaves over the entrance to my sanctuary.

Unfortunately, I was less careful than my wife. I had left my old cap on the kitchen trestle. The soldiers saw the cap and guessed I must be nearby. Lizzie told them it was an old cap she had a mind to repair for herself, as her good man was gone away. She was always a clever one, my Lizzie!

The soldiers searched the house, trashed the furniture and sliced our mattress. Frustrated, they vented vengeance on little Johnny – plunging the sick child into a bath of water.

They thrust their bayonet blades into every stack in our yard. Thrice a jab rent my shirt. Once my arm was deeply cut, but I managed to strife a cry of pain. The soldiers departed with curses, promising return in the morning. I did not want to

Waves breaking on Whitepark Bay.
Oil. 24" x 36".

At Port Braddan in 1979. Pen and ink. 16" x 12". Eamon F. Murphy.

chance a third good luck escape from the Yeomanry. I determined to follow many other fugitives to the land of freedom. I would send for Lizzie and the boy, when I had made a place for them in America.

However, I did not avoid a third confrontation. It happened this way. My friends procured a passage to Boston for me on the Glasgow Boat, which was accustomed to take on passagers from the Pan Rock at Ballycastle.[9] I schemed to lie hidden in the smugglers caves at Dunananie Castle, till my ship would come into sight.[10]

The following night was moonless and lashing with rain. On my way to Ballycastle at Milltown near Currysheskin, three soldiers accosted me, but I was determined to get to Ballycastle. I felled one of them with a blow, stuck his mate with a dagger and took to my heels, the third solider followed in hot pursuit.

Something ghostly passed secretly in the damp darkness. I hid behind a hedge. The solider followed the phantom, thinking it was me. At Araboy he discovered he was trailing an old grey donkey! I boarded the ship at Ballycastle and arrived safely at Boston Harbour after a fair voyage of thirty days.

America welcomed young Ulster Scots fugitives with open arms. Fortunes could be made in the New World. The years flew by, but Lizzie would not venture across the Atlantic Ocean. She worked our farm at Tonduff and watched young Johnny grow into his teenage years.

Then in the year 1812 the lease on our farm was due to expire. Our neighbour, that informer the blow-in from Coleraine, offered the land agent a double rent for my land. I knew it was time to come home.

By 1812 the Irish Parliament had been dissolved and the United Kingdom had come into being. Robert Peel was chief secretary for Ireland – Orange Peel as they called him! High prices resulting from the Napoleonic wars were bringing prosperity to Irish farmers. I was a wealthy man and could easily afford the price of a pardon. The events of the old century and the United Irishmen were all forgotten and we were finding the side on which our bread was buttered.

There was a great homecoming at Tonduff. Lizzie was as beautiful as the day she arrived at Tonduff from the Isle of Skye, although that was eighteen long years ago. Much had happened to me in those years, but nothing had changed in Tonduff. Like Lizzie our farm, was as beautiful as ever. Our boy John is a chip of the old Curry block. He will get the farm when old age makes Lizzie and me sit in the ingle-nook to talk over the days of 1798 on long winter nights. Spring and Summer you will find me down at Port Braddan fishing from the rocks.

Liberalitas, Aequitas, Fraternitas.[11]

AUTHORS NOTES

John Curry's letter could have been written by any of several young blades on the Causeway Coast during the latter days of the eighteenth century. Most of those who fled to the land of freedom remained there and helped to found the Untied States of America. We are fortunate that John had his loving and loyal wife, Lizzie, to call him home to tell the story of that part of the Causeway Coast history.

1.   The native Irish rebellion of 1641, against the influx of Scots and English settlers, became confused with mainland politics. On August 15, 1649 Oliver Cromwell came over to *'Mop Up'* the rising. He projected himself as liberator from Irish barbarism, royalist misrule and Roman Catholic hypocrisy! At Drogheda he massacred 3,500 in reprisal for the 1641 rising; in Waterford over 2000, while in parley with the citizens. The nine months campaign cost £3.5 million, part of which was raised by division of confiscated Irish land. Parts of Antrim, Down and Armagh were among the 14 counties seized. Punishment for those who had not supported Parliament was transportation to the colonies or Connacht for life.

2.   After defeat in England; James II continued his war in Ireland (1689 to 1691). His supporters besieged Derry (April 1 to July 31, 1689). The city population increased from 2000, to 30,000 refugees and soldiers. 1500 citizens died of disease and malnutrition.

3.   One of the ships had taken on extra provisions from Rathlin Island. The ships had sailed from Liverpool on contrary winds on May 17 1689. On June 1st they were forced into Ramsey Bay. On June 8 they joined the grand fleet in Red Bay. The Dartmouth, commanded Captain Leake, was forced by gales onto Rathlin Island on the voyage to Lough Foyle, here he took abroad 100 head of cattle.

4.   *'Hooley'* is a Derry and North Antrim word which means a evening social gathering for entertainment.

5.   At Irish fairs the agreed sale of animals was sealed by each party spitting on his palm before a hand shake.

6.   The Oath of a United Irishmen was: Question: Are you straight? Answer: I am. What have you got in your hand? A green bough. Where did it first grow? In France. Where are you going to plant it? In the Crown of Great Britain.

AUTHOR'S NOTES

7.   The Battle of Antrim took place on June 7, 1793. Sir John Clotworthy M.P. had opposed the ideas of Oliver Cromwell, encouraging Dissenters to settle in Antrim town. Their descendants raised a force of 3,500 volunteers for the United Irish Rising. Henry Joy McCracken led them into battle in the middle of the town. Although the government commander, Lord O'Neill, was killed, the rebels were routed. Later Henry Joy McCracked was hanged.

8.   Croaghmore mountain is approached by the road from White Park Bay to Mosside. It was a favourite place for hunting and shooting. It may have been a site of pre-Christian worship. The ruins of a Dissenters Kirk and the present day Presbyterian Church are nearby. In the mid eighteenth century a congregation was established under the pastorate of Bushmills church. The building, which was nearer the summit of Croagh mountain, lost its roof during the great storm of 1794. The present edifice was erected in 1830 and refurbished during the long ministry of the Rev Hamilton Henderson (1893 to 1943).

9.   The foundation of the American Republic in 1776 encouraged considerable Irish immigration. The first U.S.A. census (1790) estimated 400,000 citizens mostly Presbyterians. The Pan Rocks, at the east end of Ballycastle bay was the point from which a tender took passengers to the trans-Atlantic ship. It is the site of an old salt drying pan and a popular place for fishermen.

10.   Dunananie (Dunaynie and Duninenny) Castle. O.S. Memoirs (1835) refer to a small castle on the cliff edge, a mile west of Ballycastle. It was the earliest MacDonnell castle (c. 1500), in it Sorley Boy was born and died. In 1606 Randal MacDonnell was granted a charter to hold a market, on the site, every Thursday (hence the name 'Hill of the Fair'). The O.S. Memoirs also mention the spectacular caves at sea-level. These were used as safe hide-outs for smugglers. It seems John Curry made good use of both rocks and caves as he got away safely to start a new life in the U.S.A.

11.   Liberty, Equality, Fraternity was the rallying – cry of the French Revolution (1789). It was adopted by the United Irishmen (1798).

XI THE RECTOR'S LETTER

THE REVEREND ROBERT TRAILL M.A. BALLINTOY 1753-1842

Blessings to you. As you prefer the Presbyterian, rather than the Episcopalian system of church government, I shall commence this letter to your Mill House with my ecumenical credentials. Both Irish and Scottish branches of our family date back to Walter, Bishop of St. Andrews. That was in the fourteenth century and long before the Reformation which established a state church - Presbyterian in Scotland, Episcopal in Ireland.

William, my great grandfather, came to Ireland for ordination and became minister of Lifford in 1680. In 1684 William set sail for the American colonies and ministered in Maryland until his return home for installation in the Borthwick congregation of Dalkeith in Scotland where he died in 1714.

William's son Robert, my grandfather, was born in 1687 while the family was living in the American colonies. He became minister of Panbride in 1717. When he died in 1762, his remains were interred under the Panbride nave. His elder son Robert, my father, became minister of Panbride when my grandfather died.

My uncle James came to Ireland and was consecrated Bishop of Down and Connor in 1765. My brother Anthony became Prebendary of St Andrews in Dublin, Archdeacon of Connor and Rector of Schull in the Diocese of Cork.

For some reason best known to himself, my father dropped the second 'L' from our name. At the time the jibe was *"Robert made one 'L' of a difference to the family name"*. In Ireland we continued to spell our name with two 'Ls'.[1]

My cousin John Trail became the first minister of the Free Presbyterian Church in Scotland. For good measure let me tell you about Sister Agnes Xavier, my cousin Anne Agnes Trail, a daughter of Dr. Trail. Agnes was born in 1798 and came over to visit us in Ireland. Here she became deeply convicted of the Christian way of life. Agnes became a successful artist and eventually gave her allegiance to the Roman Catholic Church. In 1834 she helped to found the Edinburgh Convent of the Order of Ursulines of Jesus.

So, as you can see, ours is a truly ecumenical family! I am sorry that you did not have the opportunity to benefit from my ministry in Ballintoy parish. I came here well before your time at Port Braddan. However, I often sit at my study room window and look down upon that beautiful little place with the Giant's Causeway floating upon the horizon. Some evenings the setting sun makes all things golden as an ethereal back-cloth to a perfect picture.

Many a fine salmon has graced the rectory table from the nets in your little port. God was good when he gave this special corner of his vineyard for us to tend and enjoy.

I was instituted into Ballintoy Parish on August 19, 1777. It was a beautiful summer's day, as I recall, and we were in the old church. I have ministered here for nigh on sixty five years. I was a mere boy of twenty-two years in 1777 and well under the canonical age for ordination to the diaconate.[2] Only one week thereafter, I became a priest and a rector! I served no time as a curate assistant; which omissions from my education I never found a hindrance. If anything it was a positive benefit. At least a year should have passed between my ordering as deacon and priesthood. However, my uncle was the Rt. Rev. Dr. James Traill, Bishop of Connor and Patron of Ballintoy. He organised the *"Reasonable Causes"* which occasioned my extraordinary rapid promotion. My brother the Rev. Dr. Anthony Traill was vicar of Billy, of which parish Ballintoy had been a part until 1670. My brother may have had much to do with my rapid preferment!

Our little church is very beautiful, magnificently situated above the high sea cliffs and filled with friendly people. Originally it was built as the proprietary chapel of Ballintoy Castle. The Stewart family arrived on the Causeway Coast from Bute, shortly after the year 1560 and built the castle in the first decade of the seventeenth century.

At that time the parish church was at Billy. There were two burying yards and a chapel of ease at Templastragh, close to the basalt cliff, above your mill at Port Braddan. It was dedicated to Lassara and known locally as the church of the flame.[3] The importance of that ancient place diminished when the private chapel of the Stewart family became our parish church in 1670.

It seems the castle chapel cum parish church was refurbished about 1686 when the bell which Archibald Stewart donated was re-cast by his son Charles. At the same time Charles' sister, Sarah, presented to the parish our priceless chalice and paten.

In 1733, during the incumbency of Rev. Dr. Archibald Stewart, the tower was erected. It has always amused me that our tower carries a sun dial and a moon dial. The first tells the time on the occasional sunny day, the other tells the heights of the tide at Camply harbour,[4] when the moon is not covered with clouds. I never found either of them sufficiently accurate!

The tower was built by two local men, Samuel Thompson and William Finney, who received £2.13.9 for their labour. The fine tall spire, surmounted with a large golden ball and weather cock, is a beacon to sailors on the treacherous sea of Moyle. Many a fishing boat has been guided home safely into Ballintoy Port and Camply by our bell in fog, and by our shining lamp on storm lashed nights.

In 1811 I decided to refurbish the building once

Ballintoy Church

again. It had become too small for my growing congregation. I commissioned John Bowden to draw up plans for my consideration. I was dissatisfied with his drawings and asked Henry Wynne to alter the plans to my requirements. For his efforts I allowed his name to be recorded on a plaque set into the east wall. I must say he was inordinately pleased with this privilege, just as I am amply satisfied with the beautiful sanctuary he produced to the glory of God.

At that time we added the north transept and installed those tall windows with wide elliptical archivolts and multipaned glazing. In order to increase the number of pews we added the two galleries. We constructed the chancel in what had been the east end of the old building, by erecting a couple of Tuscan columns, which support the screening arch. I thought this was a clever piece of ecclesiastical architecture and much in keeping with the High Church sentiments of the times! The charming little hexagonal pulpit with its shamrock cartouche, sets off our modern building.

The work cost us over £1,400, however the Board of First Fruits[5] paid more than half of this huge sum of money. I am very skilful in persuading my congregation to part with their hard earned pennies, so the remaining money was collected quickly.

A couple of decades before we refurbished the church, I had decided that a purpose built rectory was necessary for the growing parish of Ballintoy. That was before the Traill family bought Ballylough House from Archibald Stewart. The year was 1788, but I did not move into Mount Druid until 1791. I should tell you the building of the house cost over one thousand pounds! I put up nine hundred pounds of my own money, all the Board of First Fruits would subscribe was a miserable one hundred pounds!

I chose to call my new house *"Mount Druid"* because of the proximity to a fine prehistoric dolmen. I had the option of any building site in the area. I chose the bleak hillside of Lannimore mountain, which is completely bereft of natural shelter. In 1772 my good friend, the Earl of Bristol Bishop of Derry, had selected a similar site on which to build Downhill Palace.[6] I have always thought my view over Whitepark Bay towards the Giants Causeway, is vastly superior the view from Downhill over Magilligan strand to Innishowen. As at Downhill, I enclosed a huge garden with a high wall, where vegetables and fruit trees could be cosseted into producing a reasonable harvest for the rectory table.

I built a five bay four storey stone house expertly rendered with cement in the way they call 'harled' in this area. The north-west façade has two canted bays separated by a high round headed landing window, above and below this opening are delightful little oculi. I decided to omit the six central windows from the canted bays. Outside, this gives a gelid appearance, like the surrounding countryside; inside it provides an unusually pleasing effect to the principle rooms, especially the great drawing room. I put the kitchen, scullery, wine cellar and other domestic quarters in the basement rooms. The extensive servants quarters I situated in the attics.

I was over thirty years of age when I built the glebe house, with the intention of bringing an exotic bird to sing in my golden cage. However, it was not God's will that such a happy event should be my lot, so I have spent all my bachelor days here at Mount Druid, meticulously attended by a band of faithful servants. In turn I have served them and all my parishioners for nigh on sixty five years. You ask me to describe Ballintoy during these years in which I have ministered.

Some years ago William Shaw Mason, secretary to the Board of Public Records commissioned an exact statistical account of my parish. The account is an official survey of the entire Church of Ireland, so I took considerable trouble to paint an accurate picture of Ballintoy, in the early years of the nineteenth century. The compilation made me realise how fortunately my lines have lain over all these years.

As I told you my ancestry is ecumenical. In Ballintoy we have many Dissenters and not a few Papists – with all of whom my congregation and I have the most cordial relationships. Seldom have I resorted to the manor court to enforce payment of tithes to the Established Protestant Church. The majority of the people are happy and comfortable. There are very few in poverty and charity collections alleviate their plight. There are no trouble raisers, either from political opinions or family quarrels. However, some years ago I had to send to prison that abandoned strumpet, Jane Brown of Dunseverick, who caused me considerable annoyance and encouraged others in her consummate perversity.

The people of Ballintoy are happy and healthy. We keep no resident medical physician in the parish, consequently we have no hypochondriacs! I always say, let a medico unto your patch and the ladies

will be forming a queue at his gates before his arrival.[7] Epidemic diseases appear from time to time, as in other places, but nothing that our old wives cannot cure themselves.

Small-pox is but little known these days. The former fears and prejudices against inoculation have vanished, as I took it upon myself to perform injections in my parish.[8] Many hundreds of every class and persuasion have benefited from my efforts, with complete success I am glad to say.

For these and many other reasons, longevity at Ballintoy is to be expected by our people – except for the usual tragic accidents which occur in any fishing and farming community.[9]

One annual event troubles me every spring-time, when fourteen or fifteen of our finest young people emigrate to the United States of America. I tell them *"far off fields are green, but none so green*

Mount Druid Rectory.

as the bonny fields of Carey barony". Fifty or sixty parishioners cross to Scotland for the gathering of the harvest. I am happy to say they return home joyfully, bearing their sheaves with them, in the form of a pocketful of silver.

I encourage early marriage in Ballintoy as it helps to prevent promiscuity. Over that problem I have very little supervision, no matter how much I try. To my knowledge there are forty-nine bastards in our parish and only God and the mothers know how many others!

The cottages are comfortable and clean, mostly built from stone and well thatched. Usually there are three rooms and several glazed windows. The victuals commonly used by the people are oaten-meal bread, potatoes and fish. On feast days they eat meat.[10]

I encourage the populance to dress well on the Sabbath days and holidays. The women wear muslins, calicoes, cotton stockings and splendidly coloured bonnets. Of late, I notice an umbrella is an indispensable fashion accessory, whether it is a wet or dry day! Another novelty which is an essential vogue, is the drinking of tea. As far as I can see the men of the family get little of it. However, these honest, peaceable, industrious and hospitable women always offer me a dish of tea when I call during the annual parish visitation. I always refuse the invitation as the dry tea is at six shillings a pound.

We need neither police nor magistrate in my parish. The people look to me for the control of both law and order. During the United Irishmen's Rebellion in 1798 a few hot headed youths were misled at the commencement of the uprising. Soon they saw the error of their ways and returned to their daily labours. Not a single individual of our parish joined the rebel army.

This of course occurred because I was the Captain of the Carey Yeomanry. In a single day on calling for volunteers I oversubscribed the total number required for the barony corps. Such then is our loyalty to sovereign and clergy.[11]

Before I tell you about our schools let me give you some idea of our population and how our people are employed. We have about eight hundred men and women gainfully occupied in the parish of Ballintoy.[12] There are only thirty three persons receiving aid from the various charity collections. I am sorry to tell you we have two people without the ability to speak, ten blind persons and nine denied the kindly light of reason. All these we look after most carefully.[13]

There are three houses licensed to sell spirits and two for the sale of game. We have rather indifferent fairs in the town, they cause more trouble than they provide industry.[14] For transport we have the Coleraine, Bushmills and Ballycastle post passing through every morning and returning at about five of the clock in the evening.

About half the population is Protestant, they are members of the Established Church of Ireland. There are some thousand Dissenters who are members of the Presbyterian churches at Croaghmore and Toberkeagh.[15] There is a similar number of Papists, who attend the Roman Catholic Chapel at Ballinlea.[16] I pay my curate seventy five pounds per annum. The Presbyterian clergy receive stipend and Regium Donum.[17] The priest has many sources of support which I have never been able to ascertain!

Apart from sensual pursuits, our young people have few amusements. All ages enjoy dancing into the early hours, especially on May Day and at

Christmastide. There is some cockfighting at Easter and the pagan trundling of yellow eggs down Knocksoghey Hill. Saint John's day is observed by Freemasons' processions, which like the cockfights encourage the consumption of much intoxicating liquor. The boys of the parish play football and handball. Unfortunately the private seminary at White Park House has been closed, but the splendid ball alley is still in operation. Some play the ancient game of shinty and the gentry engage in hunting.[18] In summer time the tourist trade brings many visitors to the Causeway Coast and some of our people hire out their cottages for rent.

The main coast road runs from Coleraine to Ballycastle through Ballintoy, it is in good repair but very steep. In places the views towards the sea are superb. The road through Billy to Dervock and Ballymoney crosses hilly countryside and is much improved. Also the byroads and cross-roads are well graded, all at the expense of Cary Barony. I travel all these roads myself, I have found neither impedimenta nor difficulty.

Throughout my ministry at Ballintoy I have supported the education of our young people and I hope my patronage has greatly improved the morals of the parish. You will be interested in our six schools, of which I am very proud.

The Prolisk school was built in 1831 by Dr. Adam Clark of the Methodist Society and remains under that auspices. The master receives twenty pounds per annum for teaching sixty Protestant children. A similar Methodist society school at Island Macallan has fifty nine scholars, fifty four Protestants and eight Papists.

At Lasbellanagroagh there is a private school. School master, James Hunter, who is a Dissenter, receives twelve pounds. There are forty-five scholars, thirty three Protestants and a dozen Papists, who pay about a shilling per quarter year.

At Ballinloo there is an Established Church school. The master is William Gillespie, who receives eleven pounds to teach twenty four scholars – seventeen Protestants, three Dissenters and two

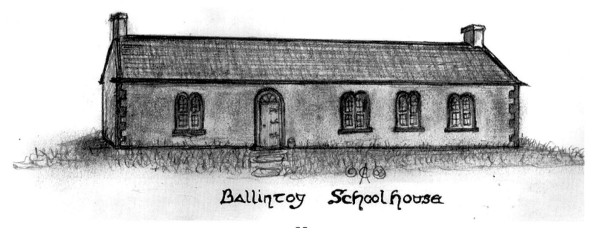

Ballintoy Schoolhouse

Papists. At Drumnagee there is another Established Church School. Here Robert Hargrave receives twelve pounds to teach twenty four children – a dozen Protestants, eight Dissenters and four Papists. The school house is hired for sixteen pounds a year.

Twenty-six scholars attend the school at Ballintoy, twenty Protestants, one Dissenter and five Papists. They pay about half a crown per quarter year to attend this school which was opened by the Established Church in 1789.

Daniel McNeill is the school master, he receives fifteen pounds per annum which is not in the gift of the Church, I am sorry to tell you. The fifteen pounds accrues from ground rents donated by Jane Stewart, sister of a previous rector of Ballintoy. That foolish woman decreed that the congregation elect, yes I say elect, the school master by majority vote! This fatuous circumstance has made our Ballintoy school the most useless of all the schools!

The only qualification necessary for the candidate is the capability to drink whiskey and share it with the electors. Whichever candidate entertains best and drinks deepest is sure to win the election! I have made many attempts to redress this serious grievance, but having been uniformly unsuccessful, I have ceased to make further effort. I think it is the only instance in which the congregation has thwarted me. Jane Stewart, Jane Brown, those silly women with their parasols and dainty dishes of tea have much for which to answer.

So now I am old and bent and grey, seldom do I rise from bed these days. My curate does the work of the parish under my strict instruction and they carry the Holy Sacrament to my bedside every week. I keep the baptism of our infants to myself. The parents bring the child to my room, here in the rectory. I celebrate the ceremony from my bed. I have christened their parents and grandparents and even a few of their great grandparents. It would be churlish and perverse to deny them the privilege of continuing the tradition to their children, while I am able to do so.

Well now, you asked me for a few words about the parish during my ministry. I hope this account has been of interest to you. In my time I have seen the reigns of five sovereigns – the three Georges, King William and her present majesty, Queen Victoria. I have witnessed the formation of the United States of America, the Irish Rebellion, the Union of the Irish and British Parliaments, Cook's voyages to Australia, Watt's invention of the steam engine, the French Revolution and the reign of Napoleon Bonaparte, the abolition of the slave trade and Catholic emancipation.

Now, equally important as any of these great events, I must prepare for the baptism of a scion of the historic Stewart family. My curate and my good house keeper will bring the parents and sponsors to my bedside and I shall read the Service, which has been so often my privilege. So a new generation comes to Ballintoy. I am looking forward to discover what happens next, when I am no longer encumbered with this ancient body and I go to meet my Maker. I believe I shall find heaven to be no strange place, as I have been living in a little corner of it all the days of my ministry in Ballintoy.

Pax Vobiscum.[19]

AUTHOR'S NOTES

On June 4, 1842 being in his eightyninth year, the Rev. Robert Traill died at *"Mount Druid"* the rectory he had built for himself, some fifty years previously. He had served as Rector of Ballintoy for sixty-five years, his only incumbency. As he wished he was laid to rest in the graveyard where he had buried so many of those to whom he had ministered. To his memory the congregation erected the fine east window in Ballintoy Church. Appropriately it depicts the Ascension of Our Lord Jesus Christ.

I have used the documentation that was available for *"The Rectors Letter"* to paint a picture of a Causeway Coast town two centuries ago. It could depict many Irish towns at that time. I included the ecumenical background of the Traill family – (Protestant/Catholic/Dissenter) as a symbol of those times. Robert Traill served his people well. This was a time when many clergy held a plurality of stipends and some seldom visited their parishes. For example the absentee Bishop of Derry (1768-1803) Earl of Bristol spent years abroad on continental travel but always came home to a great welcome from the people of Londonderry.

1. In 1814 W.S. Mason (Parocial Survey of Ireland) records the rector of Ballintoy with one "L" – Robert Trail.

2. The usual age for ordination to the rank of Deacon is twenty-three and priest twenty-four years.

3. In the Statistical Account of his parish in 1814 Rector Traill suggests the Irish derivation of Templastragh is *"Church of a horse's journey or near a waterfall"* He was not an Irish speaker!

4. Camply is the name the rector gives to the natural harbour to which the road past the church leads. He describes it as *"fit for the small craft which arrive from Scotland". It is much exposed and has a pier"*. It seems Ballintoy Port was under the coast guard's station and nearer to the Knocksoghey caves. The Rector possessed a coffee pot which had been found in one of the caves. *"An ancient brassy metal vessel with handle, spout, three legs; eight inches in height and four in width"*.

5. First Fruits. See Note 26, *"The Brigadier's Letter"*.

6. The Earl Bishop built Downhill Castle on the bleak north Derry cliffs in 1779, a couple of years later Robert Traill came to Ballintoy.

AUTHOR'S NOTES

7. *"Queue"* in 18th century sailors and soldiers wore hair in a queue (or pigtail). The word comes from Latin 'cauda' a tail.

8. Smallpox (variola). Although inoculation against this dangerous infection was practised before the Christian era, it was not till after 1800 that Edward Jenner (1749-1823) make vaccination popular in Britain. It shows the high merit of Rector Traill that he personally carried out the inoculations in his parish.

9. At that time many people in the Ballintoy parish lived to over 70 and even 90 years. One man died at 110 years of age. In 1838 Thomas Fagan reported to Ordnance Survey *"several persons above 80 live in the parish. Usual number in a family is 6. They marry early 2 recently at 15. They are prolific and twins are common".*

10. The rector listed the type of fish obtainable in his parish in 1809. Glashen, grey gannet, rock and red cod, salmon, lythe, ling, sea trout, mackerel, sea bream, haddock, grey and red garnet, roe, halebut, turbot, skate, flouder, seal, crab, lobster, and sandeels, sometimes sharkes and porpoises were to be sent. Foxes were hunted for sport as were otters in the Dunseverick river. Badgers, martens, wild cats and rats were killed especially at White Park Bay, where they did considerable mischief to the valuable rabbit population. A school of porpoises played in the bay during the summer of 2003.

11. It was usual for the clergy to hold officer status in local government forces. The Earl Bishop of Derry led the local loyal volunteers; as did Robert Traill. In Holywood one of the Dissenting clergy was a leading colonel in the United Irishmen Movement(see 'Holywood Then and Now').

12. Weavers, 228, Yeomen, 118 Fishermen, 104 Servants, 92. Tailors, 25. Cobblers, 25. Blacksmiths, 17. Huxters, 16. Masons, 13. Carpenters, 12. Fish Carriers, 10. Flax Dressers and Scutchers, 10. Basket Makers, 8, Sailors, 8. School-masters, 8. Mowers, 7. Wheelwrights, 7. Coast Guards, 7. Butchers 6. Rabbit Hunters 5. Thatchers, 5. Millers, 5. Stone Blasters, 5. Letters of Blood, 4, Pipers, 3. Reed Makers, 2. Midwives,

AUTHOR'S NOTES

2. A Fiddler, A Glazier, A Linen Merchant, A Slater, A Gardener and a Barber. I suppose the gardener looked after the grounds at the rectory.

13. Lewis (1849) recorded the population of the parish as 4816; the village had 310 residents living in 68 houses. He makes special mention of woodcoal mines in the hills behind White Park Bay (i.e Lignite). Arboreous strata were up to two feet in thickness. This fact confirms the complete arborage cover of the area in former times.

14. The *"rather indifferent"* fairs were held on June 3, September 4, and October 14 at Ballintoy Diamond and the Fair Green.

15. Rector Traill is writing this letter to the mill in the year 1842. When he made the statistical return for 1814 he recorded *"there was a Presbyterian meeting house at Croaghmore, the roof of which fell in about twenty years ago. No regular clergyman was appointed and only occasional services were performed"*.

16. During the Perscution, Mass was said at Laganaifrim. (The hollow of the mass), near the summit of Croaghmore, by Father Murray. Later private Mass Houses were used. In 1816 Ballinlea church was erected by Father Peter O'Neill. Ballintoy Church was erected in 1878 and dedicated to the Blessed Virgin and St. Joseph.

17. Regium Donum (the King's gift). A government grant towards the payment of Presbyterian clergy was initiated by Charles II in 1672. After the 1798 insurrection it was paid through a government agent and divided into three classes (£100 £70 and £50 per annum). The grant was abolished at the disestablishment of the State Church of Ireland in 1869.

18. Formerly on Christmas Day great groups assembled on White Park Bay to play 'common' or 'shinny'. Usually the day ended with broken heads and much drinking of whiskey.

19. Pax vobiscum. Peace be with you.

XII A LETTER FROM A GIANT'S CAUSEWAY GUIDE

- NELL McMULLEN THE CAUSEWAY C1880

Greetings to Your Honour and the very tip top of the morn to ye. I'm little Irish Nell McMullen, my learning is little and my skill at writing is less, but I'll be fit to write a letter to you about the Giant's Causeway, if you'll promise to take me as your guide when you come to see the world's most wonderful wonder!

I know Port Braddan very well, for many are the times I have brought my more energetic clients right around the Causeway and on to White Park Bay, to observe the great fault in the cliffs beside your mill, which divides the black basalt stone from the lovely white limestone.

I am one of the hoard of official guides who assails every tourist who appears on the road and shows a fancy to view the Giant's Causeway. I'm good at beating the others back and I like to think I have a pretty face and a winning smile for the foreigners!

We're a piebald lot, but everyone of us must be acceptable to the Agent, that is Hugh Lecky's man for the Lecky's own the Causeway, not the Antrims. Most of the guides are my cousins for the McMullen family has cornered the trade. We have Longmac, Wee Mac, Red Mac and Cockmac. The last one is so called, as his little trick is to crow like a rooster in order to amuse the party who has hired him. Miss Henry of the hotel favours poor old Dan MacWilliam, as the guide for her residents, for he has a very large family to feed. There are a few wee boys who get jobs because their fathers have died in harness.[1]

Travellers who have visited the curiosities at Killarney and Glendalough tell me the guides in those foreign places depend on lying legends, leprechauns, sad songs and absurd stories to earn their wages. We are true geologists and known all about hexagons and octagons, knowledge passed down from parent to child. We expect our clients to be astonished and that we are the astonishers! We are actors and artists and we put on a good show, so that our audience will go away satisfied. Why else would they pay us handsomely and buy our *"specimens"* from the Causeway to take home as mementos of the visit?[2]

I spend the winter months searching for examples of natural stones. Often valuable items are unearthened, even amethysts, jaspers and ambers. Some of these are placed in ornamental boxes and sold to the visitors. The hucksters, who have stalls on the road down to the Causeway, buy our better finds. We have as little as possible to do with these traders, for they are not our most favourite people!

When you come with me on the walk along the Causeway, I must ask you to be careful, as it can be a very dangerous place, especially when a high wind is blowing or someone goes too close to the cliff edge. One morning last summer, I was the first guide on the track – an early bird hoping to catch worms! I found the dead body of a women lying at the foot of the first precipice. She was young, very beautiful and well dressed in the modern fashion. Other guides arrived as the sun rose in the summer sky, and the Constabulary was called from Bushmills. However, no-one knew who she was or whence she hailed. I found a sliver of a marriage certificate in her pocket, but the names had been torn away. She had a new wedding ring on her finger. The Causeway guides took up a collection and we gave the poor girl a proper Irish wake and a descent burial, just as if she had been one of us!

Wee Jammie McMullen, a cousin of mine and a guide in training, for his Da had died recently, suffered a similar tragedy. One day he was jumping over the rocks like a jack in the box. A neighbour's child followed him and froze with fear beside a deep chasm which Jammie had jumped over with ease. Jammie, laughing at her fear, held out a helping hand, but the wee girl drew back and Jammie tumbled headlong into the raging sea below. His small mangled body was washed up on Isla in Scotland many weeks later.

But let me tell you a merry story of another wee boy. It concerns the Chimneys which beckoned the ships of the Spanish Armana to perdition. When the ailing mother of a local idiot child died, he asked the minister where she had gone. His reverence told the boy his mother had gone up to heaven. *"Gone Up"*, says he, *"as high as the Giant's Organ?"* Much higher was the reply. *"As high as the Chimneys? "Yes, and Higher"*.

The next day the neighbours found the idiot son atop the Chimneys clapping his hands and howling for his mother. They had never heard of anyone who had climbed the chimneys before that day and none could attempt the ascent now.

As the boy refused to come down some of the locals decided to keep watch through the black night, but like Our Lord's disciples they fell into a deep sleep. When the morning sun rose they saw the summit of the Chimneys was empty and the desolate keepers thought the child had fallen while they slept, They searched for hours but found no body.

Sorrowfully, they returned home to Tonduff. There they found the boy sitting on his door step. *"I could not find my mammy"* was all he would say through his tears.

You will be asking me how this wonder of the world, the Giant's Causeway, got its name. Sure,

The old Royal Hotel

104

the great Irish giant – Finn MacCool, father of our famous poet Ossian, dejected by unwonted defeat, forsook the world and hid himself away in the vast cave at Port Coon. He took a vow never again to eat food from human hands. When he was nigh death a beautiful seal swam into the cavern bringing him fish in her mouth. He recovered and built the Causeway so that he could cross to Staffa and defeat his Scottish enemy. On his way home he removed the centre of the bridge, so that he could not be followed. The Scottish and Irish ends of the Causeway remains to the present day.[3]

We guides use the story of the giant and his gate, chair, organ and ball alley, to amuse our gullible clients! Long ago the Gaels had called the strange place by the name *Clochan na bh Fomharaigh* the steeping stones of the Formorians, *"The men who came from under the sea!"*. They were one of the earliest tribes to invade the northern coast of Ireland. Before you take the walk, let me give you the scientific background to our Causeway and how it came to be a place of universal interest.

In 1692 William King, Bishop of Derry[4] stirred up public interest in the phenomenon. By 1771 French scientists became aware of the volcanic origins of the curiosity. Then in 1790 the Rev. William Hamilton published his "letters" on the natural architecture of the place. By 1834 Charles Lanyon's magnificent Antrim Coast Road was bringing visitors flocking to the Causeway in their thousands. Soon the provision of superior hotel accommodation became necessary. In 1855 the railway from Belfast reached Portrush and in 1883 a local man, W.A. Traill, opened the world's first hydro-electric tramway. Its terminus was at the Giants Causeway.[6]

In 1842 William Makepeace Thackery came to see the travellers' spectacle of which all Europe was talking. The great author called the guides *"A group of shrill beggar-boys and rough boat-men lying in wait for helpless travellers"*. More famous people had better words to write about us. The year after Thackery's attack on the guides, best seller *"Hall's Ireland"* redeemed our good name and put the Giant's Causeway on the world tourist map where it has stayed ever since.[7]

We have three magnificent caves to the west of the Causeway, cutting into the cliffs between Portnaboe and Blackrock at Runkerry House. Runkerry cavern carves into the basalt lava flow for seven hundred feet, rising

Kane's Royal Hotel c.1880.

105

to cathedral heights of sixty feet. We go there by boat from Portnaboe, before we take the walk around the headlands to your cottage at Port Braddan. On the boat trip you'll see the Pigeon cave. We can climb to Portcoon cave, but please do take care it's a very dangerous place and we don't want any accidents.[8] I have told you the story about Portcoon, now you'll see how it extends three hundred feet and reaches forty feet in height rising into a fine Gothic arch. Waves rushing into all these caves make a sepulchral and soporific sighing. The long echoes of halloos from the boatmen resound against the rock walls. A single gun shot magnifies into the roar of an invading army.

Now let me acquaint you with the simple geological structure of our Causeway. Sixty million years ago the whole expanse of North Antrim was a great limestone spread. Intense volcanic activity forced molten rock to pour out through innumerable 'fissures'. Those are long narrow cracks or openings in the limestone. The flow formed Europe's largest lava plateau.

The exposed edge of the plateau is where the lava flow met the Atlantic ocean, which has been griding down the Giant's Causeway ever since. Gleaming limestone still shines through at the White Rocks, Portballintrae and White Park Bay. There were several eruptions of black lava flow through the cracks in the white limestone, perhaps separated by millions of years. The very interesting band of bright red rock which you will see on our walk, is the weathered layer of an out flow of lava, before the next spectacular eruption of lava exploded.

The peculiar climatic conditions in which the lava cooled down and crystallized produced our famous basalt columns, some of which are ninety feet in height. Basalt covers more than half the earth's surface and was produced by the partial melting of earth's mantle. The conditions which produced the Giant's Causeway created a quarry a mile to the south of Port Braddan also the splendid scenery at Staffa in Scotland. You'll find a mini Giant's Causeway on Lanzarote and another in New Zealand.

The columns are built in blocks on the simple ball and socket principle, so closely packed together that rain water cannot penetrate, yet so distinct that a separate pillar can be removed in its full length!

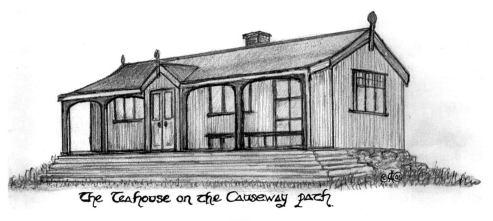

The Teahouse on the Causeway path.

Mostly the separate blocks are five or six sided, some have four sides and a very few are three or even seven sided. Of course, the three sided stones are very lucky. We call the only eight sided block "the keystone". I shall show it to you. I tell tourists to be very careful, if it is removed the Causeway will collapse!

The keystone is in the Grand Causeway, where I will show you Lord Antrim's parlour, the fan and the coffin. The famous wishing well is in the Little Causeway with the giant's grandmother always climbing, climbing, climbing for a drink of cool clean water. The honeycomb and the wishing chair are in the Middle Causeway.

Then we'll go through the Giant's Gate to see the mighty organ. It has sixty pipes stretching for forty yards and rising to the same height in the centre of the organ case.. Now we pass the kelp kilns[9] of Port Noffer[10] into Port Reostan[11] where the giant built his amphitheatre. Here is a detailed geological text book on the construction of the Causeway. I'll show you the stages of the cooling lava, millions of years ago; you'll see the upper and lower layers of columns and the ribbon of bright red ironore.[12]

Now we'll pass the giant's harp, the chimney tops, where the little idiot boy sought for his ma, and the Spanish organ. This is called Port na Spaniagh[13]. Here it was that the galleass 'Girona' broke her back on the razor rocks. She was the last ship of the Spanish Armada to perish on the Irish coast.[13] Perhaps some of the sailors were buried in the Dunluce grave yard on top the cliffs in the year 1588.

We'll go on quickly past Horseback Headland to Port na Callien[14] where the priest tends his flock and the king keeps court with his nobels. We'll drink from the well at Port na Tober and climb past Lovers' Leap to Raskin head.[15]. Here you'll behold all the three hundred and fifty feet of magnificent headland. This is my favourite view of the whole seven miles of Causeway path, from your mill to Runkerry.[16] You wouldn't believe it, but the majority of people who come to the Giant's Causeway visit only the little area between Port Ganny and Port Noffer!

However I'll not allow you to be a lazy loiterer! Ever onward, we'll past the horseshoe harbour, the murder hole and the nurse with her child. The child, like a cuckoo, is as big as the woman herself! Then at Benbane we'll see the lions head, the twins, the ball alley and the pulpits, all created in natural stone for the amusement of my party of 'visiting tourists'.

We'll stop for a picnic lunch at Hamilton's seat. Somewhat rested, we'll press on and look down upon Port na Truin[17], then pass over Bengore head[18]. Now Port na Brock[19] will appear far beneath us, then Port Fad[20] and Port Moon[21.] Each has its salmon nets, set out to trap the unfortunate fish which are heading for the River Bush to lay eggs in their ancestral shingle.[22]

Benedanir port[23] with its kelp kilns and drying walls will bring us to Dunseverick Castle and then on to Port Braddan. I hope you'll invite me into your cottage for a cup of tea or something stronger. Then you can cross my hand with silver for a full day's employ – I don't come cheap!

I hope you'll enjoy the outing I have planned for you and that you will recommend me as a guide to other *"blow-ins"* to the Causeway Coast, like your good self.

As far as I know I am the only guide who has a personal poem written by an appreciative client.[24] I'll recite it to you before I bid you a fond farewell.

Who'll buy a box of specimens just gathered from the strand?

I've Irish diamonds fit to deck the proudest in the land;

With amethysts and jasper too, that sparkle in the light,

And gems that glance like ladies' eyes, with lustre rare and bright;

The price is only half-a-crown, I really wish to sell:

Do buy a box of specimens from Little Irish Nell.

Then buy a box of specimens and take me for your guide,

I'll point out all that's to be seen along the Causeway side,

I'll lead you to the magic well and to the giant's chair

And all will surely come to pass you wish when seated there.

May the road rise to meet your feet and may your shadow never grow less.[25]

AUTHOR'S NOTES

1. An interesting Irish custom is that offspring inherit from parents the family trade or profession. Several ragged lads offered themselves as proficient guides to the Causeway because their fathers had *"died in harness"*. Sometimes the boys knew more about *"The History"* than their elders. Such patrimony was found in the church, medicine and stevedoring. Stevedors passed "the button" from generation to generation.

2. Before the National Trust acquired the Giant's Causeway and the Coastal Path for public use, the owners charged an entrance fee and provided land for traders. Tourists walked past a long line of wooden huts, all of which sold souvenirs of the Causeway Coast experience.

3. On the Scottish mainland, Fingal's cave on Staffa displays similar basaltic creations.

4. William King became Bishop of Derry in 1661, and Archbishop of Dublin in 1703.

5. After much discussion at Royal Society and University level, Rev. William Hamilton published a comprehensive account of the Causeway coast (1790). He saw the phenomenon as *"natural architecture"* or *"a work of nature"*. Hamilton's observations lost him his living and his life (1797). His name is memorialized in Hamilton's seat at Benbane Head. Dr. Samuel Johnston said *"The Causeway may be worth seeing, but not worth going to see"*.

6. In 1848 a railway from Belfast to Carrickfergus and Ballymena was opened. The line was extended to Coleraine and Portrush in 1855. W.A. Traill opened a hydro-electric tramway to Bushmills in 1883. (A world first). It was extended to the Causeway in 1887.

7. The Causeway is a World Heritage Site and attracts thousands of visitors every year.

8. Port coon – the narrow inlet. Portnaboe – the inlet of the cow.

9. See note 23 in *"The Brigadier's Letter"*.

10. Port Noffer – the giant's port.

11. Port Reostan contains a fine example of dolerite dykes and giant's eyes. The giant's harp appears in the columns which have taken on a curving appearance.

AUTHOR'S NOTES

12. It was from such a layer of ironore that the file discovered in the Port Braddan cave was filled.

13. The story is told in the letter from the Spanish Captain, Francisco De Cuellar.

14. Port na Callian – the girls' inlet.

15. Port na Tober – the inlet of the well.

16. Runkerry – promontory of the pillar – stones.

17. Port na Truin – the inlet of the stream.

18. Bengore head – peak of the goats.

19. Port na Brock – the badger's inlet.

20. Port fad – the long landing place.

21. Port Moon – possibly so called from its crescent shape. During the Second World War a plane taking off from an airstrip on the Port Moon cliffs, crashed into White Park Bay.

22. River Bush – either the turbulent or cow-like river, from the goddess who lived in it. The river generated power for the world's first electric tramway.

23. Benadanir port – the Dane's peak inlet.

24. Dr. T.C.S. Corry of Ballycastle.

25. Old Irish Farewell.

XIII A LETTER FROM A LOCAL LADY, MARY ALICE MACNAGHTEN DUNDARAVE (1867 – 1946)

Greetings. I should be pleased to scribe a short note about the way we lived at Dundarave on the Causeway Coast in the second half of the nineteenth century. Of course, I know Port Braddan, and have visited the mill house and the salmon fishery. Our friends, the Lesleys of Lesley Hill, formerly kept a house down there, as they own the fishery. If I remember correctly, they also own Templastragh church above the harbour, and much else besides.

We have our own salmon nets at Port Moon – but many a Port Braddan salmon has graced the third course of our dinner parties at Dundarave. As well as that, we have the river Bush meandering through the property. It provides excellent sport.

I was born in England, at Manchester, of all places, in 1867. My father was Sir Francis Macnaghten of the 8th Hussars. He made a name for himself in the Crimea and the Mutiny and even witnessed the charge of the Light Brigade. My mother, Lady Macnaghten, twenty years my father's junior, was the daughter of Billy Russell (1820 – 1907) the extremely distinguished war correspondent of the London *"Times"*. She was about nineteen years of age when I was born.

I am the eldest of our family. My siblings are Hilda, Edmund and Kenneth. Hilda was born at Dundarave, only fifteen months my junior. She was supposed to be a son and heir. The servants set up bonfires and tar-barrels on the driveway, in front of the house, to signal the happy event in proper style. When another mere girl arrived, the display was cancelled immediately, to show our father's disappointment.

Until I was ten years of age we lived at Lowther Lodge, Balbriggan. It was a splendid place for children. The front lawns ran down towards the seashore and to our own private bathing box.

However, Balbriggan has an extremely dangerous coastline. I remember the night *"Bell Hill"* was wrecked during an atrocious storm, immediately below our house. At first light we looked through the nursery windows to behold the corpses of the sailors washed up on our lawn! The full crew of nineteen hands was drowned that terrible night.

Another sad memory of lovely Lowther Lodge was the day our large dogs savaged a dear little pet dog, which dared to run onto our private beach. After that day my father would not have a dog about the place. Strangely he did permit my mother to keep a pet pig which wriggled up and down the servants' staircase at the back of the house.

We were all at Dundarave when my grandfather, Sir Edmund, died. He had commissioned the famous architect, Charles Lanyon, to build the great new house in 1847. They demolished the former Bushmills House, which had been erected only a decade previously by Sir Francis Macnaghten. My grandfather, all day long, sat huddled over a blazing fire in morning – room. Our night nursery was above the master bedroom; often I was kept awake by grandfather's moaning in the room below.

After Sir Edmund's death we came to live permanently at Dundarave. Mrs Phoebe Gladwin was appointed overseer of the nursery. She commanded absolute authority. A pious woman, she was very easily affected. In church her mouth resembled that of a cod-fish, when the sermon appealed to her emotional nature.

Mrs Gladwin's penchant in punishments was *"Whip-bottoms"*. The screaming victim was propelled into the night nursery, drawers lowered and a spirited spanking administered by a large red hand on a small bare bottom. We dreaded the degregation, but always gleefully spied on a sibling's discomfort.

All too soon we got to the age when a governess was required. My father appointed Miss Julia Bonorandi. She was large, dark and formidable, and wielded a wicked black ruler-stick. Frequently our knuckles were shades of blue, as a result of her merciless activity. However as I always look on the brighter side of life, the slashing prevented me biting my nails!

My father's estate agent, Richard Douglas, prized Miss Bonorandi more highly than we did. There was great rejoicing in the nursery the day he carried our governess off to Bay Head at Port Ballintrae, where many well disciplined Douglas-Bonorandis were born.

Miss Julia Johns became the replacement Dundarave governess. We were well used to child chastisement, a word which was not in Miss John's vocabulary – so we led her a merry dance and soon she departed.

A little German lady joined the succession – Anna von Reder. She was ill most of the time. The only thing she taught us was how to be secret hypochondriacs! Anna soon returned to Germany. For months I would eat nothing but rice puddings!

Next in line was Amelia Anne Hodgson. She came to us from England, an unhappy reject from the Academy of Music. Miss Hodgson was a complete disaster as a governess, even to my young mind, but she did cherish literature and harmonics. It was she who inspired in me a deep love for music and poetry. A.A. Hodgson lasted longer than our other governesses. She returned to a life of poverty in London and was killed when stepping off a red omnibus.

All our governesses were mistrusted by our old nurse. Mrs Gladwin had to come first in our fragile infantile loyalties. There was an never ending rivalry between nursery and schoolroom, much to the amusement of our maids and footmen. Phoebe Gladwin served the family for well over thirty years and was promoted to the exalted post of Housekeeper of Dundarave.

Discipline, punctuality and punctiliousness

Dúndarave.

were compulsory at Dundarave. Everyone, from my mother downwards, was required to follow the high example set by my father.

Sir Francis was an authoritative astronomer. All the clocks in the house were kept accurate by his meticulous calculations of the sun's position in the sky at noonday. In those days we did not have radio *"pips"* or *"the speaking clock"* available on the hour to tell the correct time.

Woe betide anyone who was late for morning prayers, meals or appointments. Those who were tardy for breakfast were allowed to partake of only bread and butter. A habit rapidly acquired, which has stood me in good stead ever since! To be sure of enjoying a full breakfast menu, one had to be waiting at the dining room door when the footman sounded the gong. Fortunately, most of our meals were served in the day nursery.

Discipline included regular exercise, good health, mental stimulation and obedience. My father was a brilliant mathematician and classical scholar

Dundarave Gate Lodge

in Latin, Greek and Persian. His favourite Sunday light reading was *"History of the Decline and Fall of the Roman Empire"* by Edward Gibbon. Sir Francis was an excellent equestrian and required his children to emulate his prowess. Frequently he would walk from Bushmills to Coleraine and back for some trifling item, thinking nothing of it and enjoying the exercise.

We were supposed to be neither seen nor heard. That stipulation suited us admirably! Dundarave was a very large mansion in which one could become lost for hours on end. Water, light and heat were at a premium. There was only one bathroom for scores of bedrooms and it was positioned halfway down the main staircase. Maids brought tin baths and carried hot water to the various rooms. After sun down, the vast house was illuminated by paraffin oil lamps. Rows of candle-sticks were lined on the hall table, to light the way down dark passages to cold bedrooms. Usually the draughts which whistled around the great hall gallery, extinguished the candle flames as soon as they were ignited. Few people of the present century understand the improvement the installation of electricity brought to domestic comfort.

Strangely, no-one seemed to object to a menagerie of animals in the house, as long as the collection did not include dogs! We kept cats and their kittens, hares and leverets, parrots, grouse, doves and even fish in an aquarium at the school-room door. My sister, Hilda, had a white goat called Nellie, I had a deer called Lorne. They wore coloured ribbons with bows around their necks and followed us everywhere .

We had families of dormice and squirrels. For personal amusement I always took a special little dormouse along to church with me. Frequently the squirrels escaped into the chimneys. A favourite rainy-day game was to sit on the beautiful marble mantlepiece in the drawing room, equipped with a rug to drop on the poor creatures, when they appeared from the empty fire place.

Our best pets were our ponies and the family horses. You should remember those were the days prior to motorised transportation. In fact the world's first electric tramway did not come into operation until 1883. It ran between Bushmills and Portrush. Although I do remember much discussion took place in 1873 pertinent to the construction of a narrow gauge railway line from Portrush through Bushmills to Ballycastle. It would have traversed James Leslie's land at your Port Braddan and some of our properties in Bushmills. We were sorry that nothing came of the project.

This will enable you to understand why horses were very important to our family. I owned a bay mare called Ladybird, built with the heart of a lioness and the back legs of a poodle. Hilda had a hunter called Jumbo, which had to be forced to go on the sands. One day after a fight to get him on the shore, he galloped through the high tide, fell on a submerged rock and smashed his shoulder. Jumbo had to be shot, Hilda survived. My brother Edward had a grey. It bolted from the stable yard and broke its back in the River Bush. My other brother, Francis, rode a clumsy bay with feet like oysters, we called him Doctor. Doctor had a penchant for a specific sandhill, up which he would plod without bidding, remain on top surveying the view and paying no attention to Francis. My mother rode a beautiful black mare called Galoopza. One day Galoopza ran away on the Causeway Road and did not stop till she arrived at the stable door.

As well as our favourite pets there were the carriage horses, which we rode on the sly, no doubt encouraged by the grooms and stable boys. Let me tell you that in those days every important family had a right to sport cockades on the hats of coachmen and footmen. Very soon people of no importance followed the example, so it did not count for much!

Beardiville House.

The weekly fulcrum around which family life at Dundarave centred was Sunday morning service. We were washed and dressed in our best clothes. *'Best,'* as with everything else, was chosen by our nurse and purchased in Steel's drapery shop at the top corner of Bushmills Main Street.

After Sunday breakfast our lumbering omnibus, drawn by

The Gate lodge of Beardiville House.

two fat horses, collected the house staff for the drive to Dunluce Church. The family followed in the carriage. On arrival at church we were conducted to the large square Macnaghten pew, the maids sitting in lines in the pews behind.

I spent the time of devotion playing with my pet dormouse, trying to make the servants laugh. During the sermon I read the inscriptions on the Macnaghten monuments. My favourite memorial is to a relative who accidentally set herself on fire, when striking a lucifer! The rector considered Hilda and I sufficiently well coached in theology to become Sunday school teachers. Later, I have found a greater satisfaction in the Presbyterian form of service, to which my husband introduced me.

When Charles Lanyon designed Dundarave, he included a vast square hall in the centre of the house, which ascended to the roof.. Around the hall, at first storey level there is a wide balcony. When I was about fourteen years of age my mother liked me to walk with her around the gallery, singing sacred songs. Her favourite hymn was *"Jesus Lover of My Soul"*, which, thereafter, I have always detested. Intuitively I knew disaster was imminent.

A drama which none of us could have imagined invaded the privacy of the Dundarave family. My mother, then only in her early thirties, suddenly departed. Lady Macnaghten found it necessary to be with a man called Thornhill, who was land agent to our friend Lord Macartney of Lisanoure . A faithful personal maid, Lydia Martin, departed with my mother.

My father, of whom I have always been afraid, became morose. Mother's pictures and mementos were removed. Orders were given that her name was never to be mentioned again. At this point in our lives father developed a rather strange sense of humour. On return from his frequent trips to London, he would bring back a single gift for all four of us. For the ownership of the trinket we were required to draw lots! Perhaps it was one of his many economy projects.

I did not see my mother again for a dozen years and then only after my own marriage. I visited my grandfather, Sir William Russell, at Hampton Court with whom she was living and met our half sister little Evelyn.

During those teenage years the Dowager Lady Macnaghten took an interest in her motherless grandchildren. Frequently we were sent to stay with her at 18 Eaton Square, London. There another succession of governesses taxed our undoubted ingenuity. For one unfortunate French tutor we pretended to be puppies, lapping our food off the nursery floor.

At home, for feminine friendship, father produced a Mrs Montagu – a very pretty little thing, as hard as nails, but a good horsewoman. Hilda got on well with her – I disliked her intensely. The Montagu children were unmanageable. In the hope of adhesion, they would flick butter pats at the ceiling of their day nursery! Eventually she killed a child by leaving it tied up in a cupboard, where it strangled itself. Of course, she was sent to prison. We spoke of her no more, as in the case of our mother.

Before I conclude the account of Bushmills days I should include two sad events which removed the immediate heirs to Dundarave.

Both my brothers were professional soldiers. In 1899 Edmund, my sister Hilda's favourite, was drowned in India. While changing camps, he was granted a short leave from duty. On Thursday 12th October 1899, after breakfast, he went on a fishing expedition on River Jhelum. Edmund's servant said his master had hooked a very large fish and was playing it when he was pulled into a deep pool in a rocky ravine, some two miles from camp. His corpse was retrieved an hour and a half later. Edmund was buried that evening with full military honours.

Kenneth, who was my special brother, was quartered in London with his regiment at the Tower. It seems he got into some of minor pecuniary problems. Father had no time for that sort of thing and had the poor boy sent to another battalion in Egypt. He died at Khartoum on 16th April 1903. The hospital nurse sent me a lock of his hair, which I have worn in a locket ever since, it will be buried with me.

At the close of the year 1892 my father gave me a letter from William Robert Young of Galgorm Castle. It was a proposal of marriage, of which my father approved and to which I had looked forward

Benvarden House

for several years. By this time my sister Hilda was Mrs Cecil Phillips and I was very lonely at Dundarave. Willie was a great favourite with my family. And my father pointed out – *"I was in my twenty-fifth year, it was unlikely I should have any other chance of marriage, so I had better seize this one"*.

We married in Bushmills on 28th August 1893, and took up residence in Ballymena as soon as possible. I left Dundarave behind and immediately fell in love with Galgorm Castle which I have enjoyed ever since.

In 1935 I wrote down my recollection for my grandchildren. Here I have told you about the Dundarave days. Unlike yourself my *'school-days'* were not the best of my life! The happier days came afterwards.

"Sursum Corda, Lacrimae Rerum Sunt."

AUTHORS NOTES

The Macnaghtens received land grants from Randal McDonnell when the Scottish family settled on the Causeway coast in the seventeenth century.

In 1837 Sir Francis Macnaghten built Bushmills House. Sir Edmund Charles Workman – Macnaghten replaced Bushmills House with Dundarave in 1847. Sir Francis inherited the estate in 1876. He died in 1911.

Sir Francis Macnaghten was Queen Victoria's Lieutenant for County Antrim, and Chairman of Bushmills petty sessions. When county councils were established in 1899 Sir Francis was elected to represent the area by an overall majority of votes. In 1910 the Grand Jury recognised his service to the county with the presentation of a silver cup.

Runkerry House was built in 1883 by Lord Macnaghten, brother of Sir Francis. The Giant's Causeway school-house was erected as a memorial to him. His lordship was an outstanding authority on British and Irish law.

A fuller account of the Macnaghten story is interesting. *"Randall MacDonnell appointed John Dhu Macnaghten land agent of the Antrim estates (c. 1603). John leased 60 acres at Benvarden and 60 acres at Ballymagarry where he established his residence. After his death his son Daniel removed to the more salubrious Benvarden House. Eventually Benvarden was purchased by the Montgomery family, the extravagances of John ("half-hung Macnaghten"), having devastated the estate. In order to prevent John inheriting the Beardiville property, his octogenarian uncle Edmund produced a son and heir – Francis Workman Macnaghten. Francis acquired the Bushmills estates by marriage with Letitia Dunkin and soon built Bushmills House (1837). It was demolished by their son, Edmund, in 1847 and replaced*

AUTHORS NOTES

by magnificent Dundarave. The estate passed to Sir Francis and then to Sir Edward of Runkerry House. After Edward's death in 1913, the great house came in turn to his four sons and three grandsons. When Sir Anthony died in 1972, he was succeeded by his son Sir Patrick Alexander Macnaughten".

Mrs Mary Alice Young of Dundarave and Galgorm (1867-1946) gave her life to public affairs, charitable and social welfare work. She was a member of the Ballymena Board of Guardians and Rural Council, District Nursing Society, Governor of the District Hospital and Education Committee. Mrs Young was President of the Soldiers' Sailors' and Airmen's Families Association, the U.S.P.C.A. and N.S.P.C.C. She maintained a life long association with Ballymena Musical Festival.

I have not annotated the Dundarave letter as it comes from a text written by Mrs Young, herself. Eye-witness description of "Big House" life-style in the second half of the nineteenth century is both rare and fascinating. I hope I have been able to capture something of the dry humour and unique satire of this exceptional and talented lady whose childhood was spent on the Causeway Coast.

"Sursum Corda, Lacrimae Rerum Sunt."

Be of good cheer, life is full of sorrow.
(Lift up your hearts, there are tears for things).

XIV THE BRIGADIER'S LETTER

BRIGADIER RICHARD FRANCIS O'DONNEL GAGE.
RAHTLIN ISLAND, 1897 INTO THE 20TH CENTURY

I am writing to you from the Manor House on Rathlin and I thank you for your recent letter . It has been my intention on many occasions to record the story of my island, since the days when my grandmother wrote her splendid little essay on the subject. I have not got around to effecting such a time consuming occupation until your request came for a letter to the mill house at Port Braddan. From the Manor House windows I see the gleaming cliffs of White Park Bay across the sea of Moyle; so I shall be happy to jot down a few words on our history from my side of the water for your readers at Templastragh.

The Rathlin story symbolizes the history of the Province, every facet of life on the mainland is mirrored on the island, though usually at a later date! Not many little islands get a special mention in early world history. Gaius Pliny in his famous Naturalis Historia gives the name *Ricina* to our island.[1] Claudius Ptolemy refers to it under the same title in his Guide to Georgraphy.[2] The Greek and Latin came from the Irish *'Reachlainn'* of which the derivation is obscure. Perhaps it contains the Celtic root *'Rhygnu'* meaning to scrape – or *"The Rugged Island"* – which is an apt description of both island and people, as you will surely known.

Let me take you for a walk through our history. As far back as 800 B.C., the Neolithic factory at Brockley in Ballygill townland was manufacturing fine axe-heads and beautifully polished ceremonial stones. These carried the Rathlin trade-mark all over the British Islands. The axe-heads were made from porcellanite, one of the worlds toughest ferrous stones. How our early ancestors discovered the unique outcrop is a complete mystery. Your secret at White park Bay is nodules of flint which break open to reveal clusters of sparkling lavender amethysts. Our Rathlin secret is porcellante.

Brockley is a couple of kilometres to the north-west of the manor house. Perhaps your early White Park Bay neighbours reached the Irish mainland by way of Rathlin Head. You know our legendary connections with the children of Lir, sorrowful Deirdre, the waters of Moyle and the stark hills of Kintyre.

The island's sea-level fortifications date back beyond 1000 B.C., but our first locally recorded date is AD 580, when Comgall of Bangor Abbey sought on Rathlin solitary retreat from the cares of the world.. The islanders did not appreciate the importance of this holy man and thirty of them ganged together to fend off invaders! Comgall, never one to admit defeat, persisted and successfully established a settlement at Teampall Cooil.[3]

For some reason Irish saints were very partial to remote islands. St. Legeus followed Comgall's good example by building an abbey under the rule of Bangor. Fifty years later St. Sigenius built our first parish church. The famous St Columcille honoured the island with his presence and you can find for yourself the long list of Rathlin abbots in the Annals of the Four Masters.[4]

When you are visiting the axe factory, walk a

kilometre to the south-west and you will find the site of the church of Ruan. Search very carefully and you will discover the remains of a an enclosure guarding several stone wall circles. This is very similar to the County Down settlements where the Rule of Bangor was observed. They may indicate the Bangor Abbey foundation on Rathlin[5]. Certainly the island rectorial tithes belonged to Bangor Abbey until Henry VIII dissolved the Irish monasteries in 1541.[6]

When King James I gave North Down to Sir James Hamilton in 1609, the Rathlin tithes were included in the grant. Later the tithes were transferred to the Earl of Antrim; but that is many years ahead in our Rathlin yarn!

When you are up there at Brockley you will find one of the old graveyards, the Rathlin sweat house[7] and Dunmore Fort, a most impressive site; so take a picnic lunch with you and make a special day of your visit.[8]

Now we shall go back to the year when the Vikings made their first attack on Rathlin[9]. These Scandinavian adventures plundered the religious settlement and came back for a second helping.[10]

The final disastrous Viking attack completely destroyed the Rathlin community and left the island reeling and unprepared for the next onslaught.[11]

That incursion came in the monumental year 1177. It heralded the Anglo-Norman invasion of Ulster under John de Courcy.[12] The springtime of that year brought the immensely successful conquest to Dal Riata of which Rathlin Island was an integral part. The De Courcy regime built a fine castle on double outcrops of black basalt at the island's east point. The keep was on the outer stackrock. It was divided from the bailey by a fortified gully. This ingenious architectural achievement must have seemed miraculous to the islanders. Rathlin Castle was comparable to early Dunluce – another Norman essay. Both had a superb situation for defence, sheer cliffs descending to the ever turbulent Sea of Moyle. Alas, today, only a stone wall of an outer earthwork remains.

When John de Courcy fell from royal favour, his rival, Hugh de Lacy became the flavour of a new century. He also fell from grace and in 1213 King John granted Rathlin Castle to Duncan of Galloway. In 1216 the King restored it to the De

Rathlin Manor House.

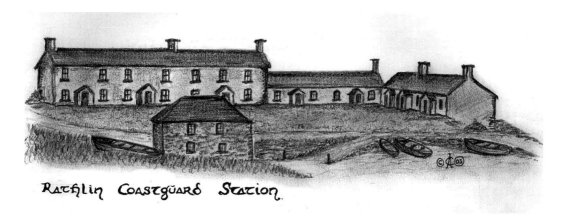

Rathlin Coastguard Station.

Lacys, Earls of Ulster. In 1242 brothers John and Walter Bisset fled to Ireland, they were exiled from Scotland as a punishment for murdering Patrick Galloway at Haddington. The Bisset family settled in the Glynns and on Rathlin Island with permission of the Earl of Ulster. At that time Rathlin Castle had a valuation of £4.8s.5d, a considerable fortune in the mid thirteenth century.

The next celebrity to visit our island was another refugee from Scotland. Although he stayed with us for a single winter (1306-1307) he gave his name to the hundred year old castle!

Robert Bruce, Earl of Carrick, espoused the ever popular cause of Scottish independence and was crowned King Robert I in March 1306. Edward I, King of England (1272 to 1307). thought otherwise and royal representatives thoroughly trounced Bruce at Methven.[13] Bruce took to the waves and sought refuge on Rathlin. The inhabitants were aghast and immediately corralled the castle and locked up their valuables. Bruce convinced them he came in peace to seek sanctuary. Squire Hugh Bisset gave Bruce permission to sojourn in the castle.

It was during that atrocious winter that the Bruce legend arose. The fugitive king was hiding in the cave beneath the castle when he saw a spider hanging by a thread from the roof, attempting to ascend its thread time after time. At last, the spider achieved its purpose and gained the safety of the cave roof. The patience and perseverance of the spider encouraged Bruce to make another attempt to free his kingdom. Returning to Scotland during the springtime of the following year he won the battle of Loudoun in Ayrshire.[14] His major victory at Bannockburn on June 14, 1314 assured Scottish independence. As punishment for the stupidity of sheltering Bruce, the Bisset family forfeited the island. In 1319 Rathlin was granted to Sir John De Athy by Edward II; however the Bissets soon regained their beloved island.

John Bisset, fifth in line from John the outlaw, died as a result of a brawl with neighbours. His only child and sole heir was the lovely Margery. She had married John Mor MacDonnell. One result of this matrimonial union was certification of the MacDonnells' clear claim to the Bisset property in Ireland. The Antrim MacDonnells acquired Rathlin Island. So by 1551 the clan held sway from the

Route to the Glynns, in which golden crown our island was an emerald jewel.

The Sassanacks suspected the intentions of the proud MacDonnell clan and in that year sent an expedition under Sir James Croft, to investigate Rathlin Island. The English were given a sound hiding, only their leader was spared to be used as a hostage for Sorley Boy MacDonnell, who was imprisoned in Dublin castle at that time!

Six years later the English sought revenge. The Earl of Sussex was government representative. His deputy, Sir Henry Sidney reported *"We landed and encamped on Rathlin until we had spoiled the same, all mankind, corn and cattle in it"*.

I suppose you could call this the Sussex massacre. The Essex and the Campbell massacres followed soon afterwards. We learned how to survive!

On July 26, 1575, Elizabeth I, being Queen, the Earl of Essex ordered the sacking and plundering of Rathlin. The Virgin Queen had offered to Essex all the MacDonnell lands, if only he could rid her of that Irish trouble raiser, Sorley Boy MacDonnell. Unable to triumph on the mainland, Essex spat fury at our island, to which Sorley Boy had sent hundreds of women and children for safety. With young army captain John Norris on board, famous navigator Francis Drake sailed three frigates from Carrickfergus to attack Rathlin Castle.[16]. Essex reported to the Queen *"There were slain that came out of the castle of all sorts – 200; and 400 more found in the caves"*. The Queen replied *"The taking of Raughlins and such Scottes as do infest our realm of Ireland and your proceedings versus Sorley Boy MacDonnell is happy success. Let John Norrice know that we shall not be unmindful of his service"*. Essex attempted to hold the island but soon found

that intention quite futile.

After the Essex massacre, Rathlin was uninhabited for some time – an island of ghosts. About 1580 Colonel McDonald and a party of Highlanders escaping from the Irish McQuillans, were forced to land on Rathlin. They found the island without inhabitants or even provisions of any sort! I like to think it was at this time that Captain Francisco de Cuellar, formerly captain of the San Pedro, a ship of the Spanish Armada, sought refuge on Rathlin Island. He recorded *"The wreched boat on which we escaped was forced on shore for two days"*. *With good weather we left for Scotland"*.[17] The next mention in history is 1637 when the Marquis of Antrim was forced to assign

East Light-House

122

"The Barony of Cary, the Lordship of Ballycastle and the island of Rachlins" to cover his monumental debts.

Then came the Irish rebellion of 1641. Charles I of the Scottish House of Stuart was on the throne. He appointed the Marquis of Argyle to be the Governor of Rathlin and sent Colonel Sir Duncan Campbell to quell the Irish island. Campbell's regiment landed in April 1642. The island men were massacred beside the harbour at Lack-na-vista-vor *"The Hallow of Defeat"*. From the nearby hill, Crock-na-screidlin, *"The Hill of Screeching"* wives and children watched the slaughter. When the women fled, the soldiers followed and hurled their living bodies over the cliffs at Port-na-Calliagh. This atrocity made the name Campbell a bogeyman to terrify Rathlin children for ever afterwards.

Next came the Commonwealth period of Oliver Cromwell. Rathlin had been assigned to trustees since 1637. As a result of the Earl of Antrim's activities during the Irish rebellion in 1641, the island was declared forfeit to the Government.

Of course, our island survived yet again. A happier event occurred in June 1689. Captain George Rooke was forced to shelter his fleet in Church Bay, while en voyage to relieve the siege of Derry. He took the opportunity to embark a herd of cattle to feed the starving defenders of the Maiden City.

When the Kingdom was re-established under Charles II, the estates of the Earl of Antrim were restored.[18] However, by 1746, MacDonnell family debts were mounting again and parcels of land had to be put up for sale. The fifth Earl, Alexander, sold Rathlin Island to my ancestor, the Reverend John Gage. He was educated at Foyle College, Londonderry and Trinity College, Dublin. He became Prebendary of Aghadowey[19], Chaplain to Queen Anne and to the Lord Lieutenant of Ireland. In 1733 John Gage married Susanna, daughter and heiress of the Rev I. Johnston of Donegal.

So it was in the year 1746, during the reign of King George II, my family became Proprietors of Rathlin. Rev John Gage died in 1763 and was succeeded by his eldest son, Robert Gage, J.P. High Sheriff for County Antrim.

When the United Irishmen were proclaiming Liberty, Equality and Fraternity throughout the Kingdom, the rising received little support on Rathlin Island. Thomas Russell, a leader in the movement and librarian of the Linen Hall Library,[20] visited the island pretending an interest in the study of geology! Assisted by Black Bob, the local priest, Father Edward McMullan, Russell urged the islanders to join the rebellion. Some even took the secret oath in Bracken's Cave, on the shore near the castle.[21] However, none crossed to the mainland to show the colour of the green flag of freedom.

High Sheriff Robert Gage died in 1801. His third son succeeded in 1804 when he was only fourteen years of age, brothers John and Frederick having predeceased Robert. Until my great-grandfather reached his majority, the estate was in the care of an agent. In 1810 Robert took up residence and two years later brought Catherine Boyd to lessen his solitude and share the island life. Catherine was the daughter of Ezekiel Boyd of Ballycastle Manor House and was accustomed to a comfortable life-style, so Robert refurbished the Rathlin house for his bride. Modern window sashes repulsed the hurricanes which howl around the island, additional flues challenged the chills, new rooms were added to make provision for a growing household – Robert and Catherine were to make the full dozen in the family way!

Their first child, young Robert, first saw the light of day in 1813. Soon the rafters of the Manor House were ringing with the happy laughter of four sons and eight daughters. A new staircase was required, marble mantels, architraves and moulding were added to adorn the plain old walls. In 1831 a new kitchen was built, no doubt to facilitate the huge family.

Robert decided to follow the calling of his grandfather and great grandfather into the ministry of the Established Church of Ireland. He had been educated at Foyle College, he entered Trinity College Dublin in 1805 aged 14, and graduated in 1810. As we have seen this was the same year in which he had taken up residence on the island. He was ordained Priest in 1818 and became Rector of Rathlin in 1824, which cure he held until his death in 1862.

My great grandfather, Rev. Robert Gage, was a propitious pastor and peerless proprietor to his people. As the island's Justice of the Peace his magisterial judgements were faultless.

During his administration the great Irish potato famine occurred. In other places landlords were creating havoc among the starving poor. On Rathlin the rents and food fees in lieu of rent, were cancelled for the duration. Proprietor Gage contributed generously to the food supplies which were imported from Ballycastle quay. The sloop *"Annie"* brought over thirty-two barrels of India corn-meal, three tons of Caroline rice and two tons of patua. Robert Gage paid the bill for fifty pounds out of his own pocket. No Rathlin Islander died of starvation during the famine years and none was evicted.[22] However, emigration from Ireland was the flavour of the time. In 1841 the island population was over

St Thomas' Church, Rathlin

one thousand inhabitants, by 1850 it had declined to seven hundred and by 1950 only one hundred people lived on the island. Population has remained about that level ever since.

During these years the main occupations of the islanders were fishing, kelp making[25] spinning, limestone quarrying, production of potatoes and barley. Perhaps even fine Rathlin sand was exported for the manufacture of Venetian glass. For a short time boat building was popular. There was one mill situated at the south end of church bay. Robert provided two store houses, one at Church Bay the other near Bracken's Cave. Weighing machines accounted all goods for trade, which mostly was with Scotland. In times of difficulty Robert accepted grain in lieu of rent, which was stored in the great barns. A particularly fine kelp store was provided on the shore beside the inn. Weaving had been introduced but it was not successful. What became a great success was Robert's battle to abolish the illicit distillation of poteen, which was destroying family life. As local magistrate he ordered the destruction of every still. As an islander himself a knew every nook and cranny where

124

apparatus could be hidden. If the distillers continued their habit they were deported to Ballycastle! This was the most severe punishment imaginable, as the mainland was regarded as a foreign country! The worst Rathlin curse is *"may Ireland be your latter end!"*

The Rev. Robert Gage was a modern man, his support for education was optimal. A scholar himself, he wanted to give the children of the island every opportunity for advance.

It seems the first school was established in 1728, eight years before Robert's grandfather bought the island. Rev. John Martin was minister at that time, in fact he was the first rector of Rathlin after the separation of the parish from Ballintoy in 1723. An interesting memorial on the south wall of St Thomas' Church, records his service to Rathlin. Daniel McNeill was the first school master, he received five pounds per annum for his tutorial efforts. The arrangement continued until 1795, when peripatetic teachers came over for the summer months. This was completely unsatisfactory, as were many of the instructors! After Robert became curate of Rathlin in 1822, he built a new schoolhouse for boys, at his own expense. It was on the old school site, close to the Manor House. In 1826 he built a girls' school in Craigmacagan townland at Ouig – to the east of the inn.

In the same year a girls' school was established in the western arm of the island, followed in 1834 by a school for boys in Ballygill south, about a third of a mile from the axe factory. Within a dozen years, from the summer season invasion by itinerant pedagogues, Robert Gage had organised four recognised schools in his parish. Parents were eager for the education of their offspring, even building with their own hands the second school for boys.

Of course, viability of a school depends upon number of students in attendance. As the population decreased, by 1875 only two schools remained open. Soon attendance figures required that even these be amalgamated. School master Harbinson became teacher of boys and girls. Schoolmistress Archer retired. By the turn of the century the school was vested in the Diocesan Board of Education.

When Robert became proprietor of Rathlin, Rev. James Moore had been rector for thirty seven years and was approaching his four score years and ten! The church building was so dilapidated that refurbishment was impossible. The rectory was uninhabitable. There were badly cracked walls, decayed floors and leaking roofs. Also, no one could find the valuable library donated by Bishop Hutchinson for the use of the incumbent![25] Rev. James Moore had traversed the Slough of Despond. His son James, an army officer, sold out to raise money for his poor sister Mary and died soon afterwards; son Hugh died about the same time. Then on May 2, 1822 his remaining son Richard shot himself in the rectory, while the family was at Church. On a Belfast almaneck for 1824, someone wrote *"Mr Moore died on March 27. He was in many ways an unsatisfactory pastor. Through carelessness and indifference by 1812 the Protestant population was reduced to about fifty"*. Robert was induced rector of Rathlin three weeks after Mr Moore's death.

Robert had become Proprietor of Rathlin in 1810. His first duty was to erect a new Church. The old building was tumbled, the replacement was completed in 1815, the Board of First Fruits contributing £738 towards the cost.[26] The building is simply constructed with limestone and basalt blocks, the fine clear glass windows have Georgian glazing. The east window is exceptionally beautiful. The tower rises to fifty feet and carries a bell by James McLaren of Glasgow[27]

Robert had no need of a rectory, the Manor House was his official residence as Proprietor. The old rectory with all its ghosts was tumbled in 1824. *"The Cottage"* was built for the curates. Robert's successor occupied the large house at Ballynoe townland, a couple of hundred yards to the west of Bracken's Cave. In 1871 'The Cottage' was elevated to rectory status, completely free of rent. In 1822 Robert's mother had provided a fifteen acre glebeland for the church. At the disestablishment of the State Church the glebe was bought by my grandfather and bequeathed to the parish, when he died in 1892.[28]

Now let me tell you about our family's long forte with the sea. In 1758 Robert's grandfather petitioned the Irish Parliament on the advantages of a lighthouse for his island.[29] The Copelands and Howth Head lights protected shipping in the Irish sea. A Rathlin light with another on Tory Island would serve the same purpose on the north coast.

As usual, Parliament listened but did nothing. It was not until 1849 seventeen thousand pounds was put into the Irish budget to build the East Light. Long after Robert's time the Bull started to flash its red eye over the sea of Moyle. During wartime a temporary light had been established at Rue Point.[30]

The 1758 petition requested that good harbours be built in Church Bay and at Ushet point – to cost £8000. Like the entreaty for a lighthouse, the provision of harbours fell on deaf Dublin ears. Again came grandson Robert with persuasion for positive action. In 1821 the first Rathlin quay was built to service a new coastguard station. The station was the answer to an urgent request for government action against piracy. Smuggling and illicit distillation were rampant when Robert became proprietor. Even today you can find one of the smugglers cottages down beside the rue lighthouse.

I have centred the Rathlin story around my great-grandparents. After a talented and meticulous pastorate and Proprietorship, Rev. Robert Gage died on his beloved Rathlin Island.[31] Catherine predeceased her husband by a decade. Robert erected a fine marble memorial to Catherine on the north wall of St. Thomas' church. Their children, John and Margaret, are also recorded on the tablet.

Before I relate the happenings of the past hundred years, I should record the story of the

Church of the Immaculate Conception.

Catholic Church on Rathlin. You know all about our connections with Bangor Abbey from AD 580 to the Viking massacres and annihilation of the Church in 1038. It seems after that date Mass was celebrated in at least three places on the island. First at Ballynagard, close to the present church, under an overhanging rock. Then at Kilpatrick, close to the old graveyard on a large flat stone. Also at Lagnasassanach, the English man's hallow, in Knockans.[32]

When Rathlin Castle was erected by John de Courcy or his representatives, a chapel of ease or a mass house would have been provided for the garrison. Several places incorporate the nomenclature 'Kirk'. The taxation of Pope Nicholas (1306) does not cite Rathlin as a separate parish. The Ulster Visitation (1622) reports *"no vicar or curate, as the island is unable to maintain one"*. The Regal Visitation (1633) records *"no vicar"* the Registrar of Priests (1704) repeats *"No Priest"*. I give you the dates for the sake of clarity.

In 1740 Friar Dominick Bradley arrived on Rathlin. By 1766 the parish priest from Armoy came over to celebrate Mass, once a month. In 1782 Father Matthew McLarnon arrived to minister to the 140 catholic families. A new church building was necessary; in 1785 Father Charles McAuley laid a twelve pence tax on every person above sixteen years of age in order to build the new Mass House. Had the parishioners been able to pay the tax, it would have brought into the ecclesiastical coffers about fifty pounds! The project was unsuccessful. The next priest was Black Ned, Father Edward McMullan whom you have already met in our Rathlin story.

About the year 1810 Alexander McDonnell purchased an old mill from the Rev. Robert Gage

for conversion into a church by the resident priest – Father Neal Loughery.[33] As the congregation increased a gallery was added – built from the timbers of wrecked ships. The congregation continued to grow and in 1865 a purpose built church was erected during the ministry of Father Michael McCartan. It is a simple building of brown basalt, a fine high timbered roof with trusses, and a pleasing little bell-cote. Each wall carries four lancet windows, the fine east window was added in 1906, a gallery in 1930. The adjacent parochial house was built in 1887.

In that very year Rathlin ceased to be a separate parish and administrators were appointed for a year's ministry at a time. For a decade, after 1909, independent parish status was returned and during this time the church hall was built. Since 1934, curates from Ballycastle administrate the parish of Rathlin.

Throughout the centuries I must tell you that both traditions on the island have lived together in peace and shared poverty and plenty as it came. As an example of this I tell you about a former priest – Father Francis McKenny[34]. Because he celebrated marriage between a Catholic and a Protestant, Father Francis had to flee to the United States, where he died after years of missionary service. He was highly respected among the island families.

Now I come to the final paragraphs of this Rathlin saga.

Rev Robert Gage was succeeded as Proprietor by my great uncle, Robert Gage, Justice of the Peace. Like all of us, he loved his island and cared for our people. He died in the Manor House in 1891 and was succeeded by his brother, my grandfather, Major General Ezekiel Gage of the Madras Staff Corps. He did not come over to the Manor but continued to live in Raghery House, Ballycastle, where he died in 1906.

By the General's will the Proprietorship of Rathlin was divided among his four sons, three of whom sold their parts of the inheritance. Unfortunately, my uncles did not sell to my father but to Mr Johnson, an Englishman who had been quarrying the limestone on the north shore of Church Bay.

My father, Captain Richard Stewart Gage, was born in India, educated at Rugby School and served in Egypt and Africa with the Royal Dublin Fusiliers. He married my mother, Norah Lillian, daughter of O'Donnell Grimshaw, at Knockbreda in 1895. My parents looked forward to a long and happy life, but, in 1909, my father was shot accidentally, when he was climbing over a wall, close to the entrance of the East Lighthouse.

My mother assumed responsibility for the Rathlin interests. In 1930 the Land Commission purchased the lands outright, leaving us in possession of the Manor House, "The Cottage" and a few other buildings.[35]

I first saw the light of day in1897 while my mother was living in Dublin. They sent me over to Wellington College. I was commissioned in the Royal Engineers in 1915. After the war I married Marjorie, daughter of Captain Conn Alexander, the uncle of Field-Marshal Lord Alexander. Every year Marjorie and I look forward to summer time visits to our island, which is never far from our hearts and thoughts.

I hope I have been able to introduce you to the long story of Rathlin. I know you have visited our island on many occasions. Come again soon.

May you live long and enjoy your mill at Port Braddan beside the beautiful White Park Bay.

"Courage Sans Peur"[36]

The Mosside Pump

AUTHOR'S NOTES

The first time I visited Rathlin Island was in company with a tent and two other students. We crossed the Sloch-na-Mara and thought of Brecain and his fifty curraghs which sank in the vortex. The mail boat was called King George V, boarded when a high wave raised the gunwale to the same height as the Ballycastle quayside.

We set up camp beside the sea in a little valley south of the castle and Marconi's test site.[37] We roamed the island for a fortnight, drank the thick cream milk[38], devoured the shop's cordon bleu pork and enjoyed the hospitality of the public house. I returned many times to stay in the Rectory, traverse the perilous cliff paths,[39] and be mesmerized by Rathlin's legends told by the world's most hospitable people. Times have changed around Church Bay[40]. The rest of the island preserves its ancient secrets for those who will always return to the Irish Kingdom of Rathlin[41].

1.   Pliny, AD 23 to 79.

2.   Ptolemy, AD 90 to 168. Both Pliny and Ptolmey may have based their comments on the records of Pyheas who sailed these waters in the fourth century B.C.

3.   Tempall Cooil –Church of Comgall (c. 580).

4.   The Annals of the Four Masters (or Kings of Ireland) is the ultimate compilation of many earlier records and was scribed between 1632 and 1636. See St. Columcille (521 to 597) and List of Abbots of Rathlin (734 to 973).

5.   The severe Rule of Bangor was lived out in circular wattle huts which surrounded a chapel with refectory, possibly a school, scriptorium and hospice. The monks lived in mixed age groups which continually offered praise in rotation. (See "Holywood Then and Now").

6.   Between 1537 and 1541 Henry VIII dissolved the Irish monasteries. In 1536 he became head of the Church of Ireland and in 1541 King of Ireland. Church lands were used as bait to win support for the Reformation.

7.   Sweat houses were used as a cure for rheumatism. Possibly this is a survivor of a beehive hut and served the purpose of a sauna. It was in use in the nineteenth century. A second sweat house was situated close to the East Light.

AUTHOR'S NOTES

8. Dunmore is situated in a valley near the highest point of the island (c.1000 B.C.) On a circular hill some 70 feet high are traces of a building (30ft x 40ft) with walls eleven feet thick. Possibly this is the legendary shining white Castle of Rathlin. It is a site of paramount importance.

9. AD 795.

10. AD 973.

11. AD 1036.

12. John de Courcy was a Norman Knight of Henry II's invasion (1171) and took Ulster by storm (1177). (See *"Holywood Then and Now"*). In Ulster he built two cathedrals, five monasteries, and 91 churches. His major contribution to English security was the ring of defensive castles, one of which was situated on Rathlin Island.

13. Robert Bruce was crowned King of Scotland at Scone (1306). His supporters were easily defeated by Aymer de Valence. Bruce escaped to Rathlin.

14. AD 1399.

15. AD 1476.

16. Francis Drake (1540 – 1596) commanded *'Falcon'* one of the 3 frigates (recently returned from the West Indies) which Essex acquired for the attack on Rathlin. Under secret instructions, the ships sailed from Carrickfergus on July 20, 1577. Siege was laid to Rathlin castle, which was partly breached on July 25. Safe passage was agreed for surrender. When the garrison appeared, utter butchery ensued. The bodies were thrown into a swamp to the west of the castle. The story is graphically told by Wallace Clark in his excellent book on Rathlin. On December 30, 1577, Drake sailed from Plymouth to circumnavigate the world, returning on September 26, 1580.

17. DeCuellar arrived at Dunluce castle in January 1589 and escaped to Scotland by boat the following March. (See 'The Spanish Captain's letter').

18. 1662.

AUTHOR'S NOTES

19.   1725 to 1763.

20.   Thomas Russell (1767 to 1803). British army officer in India (1783 to 1787) Justice of the Peace in Tyrone (1791 to 1792). Librarian of the Linehall Library (1794). He became organiser and *emissary* of the United Irish Movement, detained sans trial (1796 – 1801) organised Robert Emmet's *"insurrection"* (1803) was arrested and hanged at Downpatrick Gaol (1803) (The man from God knows where).

21.   Bracken's Cave is named from Breckan, Prince of Norway who was drowned while courting the daughter of the King of Rathlin. His dog dragged the corpse ashore. He was buried in the cave.

22.   Between 1300 and 1900 there were 30 severe famines in Ireland. Between 1845 and 1849 the potato crop was ruined on 3 occasions by blight. One million people died. In one year (1849) ninety thousand families were evicted by landlords. The population of Ireland decreased by 20% between 1845 to 1857.

23.   Kelp is obtained by burning dry seaweed in a kiln. An acid-neutralizing chemical, soluable in water, accumulates on the kiln floor. This solidifies into a bluish mass, which is used for linen bleaching, iodine etc. In 1784 one hundred tons were exported from Rathlin. As on the mainland, the May fleece or fringe brings in a vast harvest of seaweed to the seashore.

24.   1810.

25.   1720.

26.   First Fruits. Formerly dues paid to the Crown representing the first years income of a cure or parish. Dean Swift negotiated a Board of First Fruits to fund the building or repair of churches and glebes. It received parliamentary grants and was taken over by the Ecclesiastical Commissioners in 1833.

27.   1843 The bell cost £16.15.0

28.   The State Church of Ireland was disestablished in 1869.

29. Technically, Northern Ireland was ruled from the time of the Normal Conquest (1177) by Westminster. The first documented Irish (Dublin) parliament (from parliamentum *'a parly'*) met in 1264. It was followed by Irish parliaments at Kilkenny, Drogheda, Dublin etc. Dublin rule ceased in 1800, when direct rule within a United Kingdom was established at Westminster. The southern 26 counties established an independent Dublin parliament in 1922. A provincial parliament was created in Belfast for the six northern counties. Direct rule for these six counties was reintroduced for periods in 1972 and 2002.

30. Bull lighthouse 1917 and Rue Point light 1915.

31. September 29, 1862.

32. The Sassanach's Hollow. It seems an Englishman operated a blacksmith's forge in this place at some time.

33. 1816.

34. 1844 to 1846.

35. The Land Commission was established in 1881 with government grants, whereby tenant farmers could buy their land over a long period. It introduced free sale, fixing of tenure and fair rents. It was one of the greatest changes in Irish history and amounted to a bloodless revolution.

36. The Gage armorial bearings. Motto "Courage without Fear". Crest, Ram walking to the right, argent, armed. Arms, a saltire (diagonal cross) red. Argent and azure.

37. Lloyds established a signal system on Torr Head in the 1890's and soon found that Rathlin was a better location. In 1898 Marconi experimented successfully *"with a radio link"* between Rathlin and White Lodge, in Ballycastle. The Post Office objected, but in 1905 requested the Marconi company to run the service. The site of the shed where Marconi, Kemp and John Cecil, worked is marked with a few concrete blocks, adjacent to the East Light.

38. The farmers wife told us *"you get none of your mainland whitewash on Rathlin"*.

39. The secret paths were used to bring up booty from wrecked ships of which many name

plates are preserved in the Inn. The paths provided access to the nests of seagulls. Each family had its own nest patch to provide free eggs! Firewood from wrecked ships was precious, as there is no coal on the island. The best wood from the wrecks was used to carve model yachts for the Regatta which is held annually on Ushet Lough

40.   A Wind farm has been introduced to provide electricity and even street lighting. New houses are being erected for sale to people from the mainland. A mains water supply is projected. A fast, safe and weatherproof sea service has been provided and sometimes a connection with Scotland. Island roads have been improved and cars are more numerous (with the advantage of no M.O.T.tests).

41.   In 1617 a Scott, Crawford of Lisnorris, issued claims v. Randal MacDonnell that James IV had granted Rathlin to his family in 1500. The court arguments were lengthy and amusing. One of Randal's points was that there were no snakes on the island! In the end Crawford lost the case, which is recorded by Rev. G.Hill (Coleraine Chronicle) and retold by Wallace Clark in 'Rathlin Disputed Island'.

The Bishop's Urn

XV A LETTER FROM THE RECTOR'S DAUGHTER

VIVIENNE DRAPER. LISNAGUNOGUE 1922 – 1933

My parents, Albert Oswald Draper and Constance Mary Garland, were married at Dalkey in the year Dublin was celebrating the signing of the armistice which ended the first world war.

Grandfather, on my mother's side of our family had been a cattle and horse auctioneer. She used to tell us *"had it not been for the drink we should all have been very rich!"* which certainly we were not, but we knew nothing about that, in those simple days of long ago.

Mother had been the organist in Blessington, the church in which my father was curate. They fell in love at first sight and soon were married. Father's family lived at Blackrock, he had been a school master before taking Holy Orders.

Father's ability to manage teenagers urged the Bishop to assign a parish in turbulent Belfast. So we came North to St Luke's' church in Townsend Street, between the Shankill and the Falls. The rectory was a vast Victorian mansion on Ballysillan Road. It was my first home.

Industrial Belfast was a culture shock after rural Wicklow. When the Draper children started to arrive, the Bishop of Down and Connor appointed Father to St. Gobban's at Seago and then to Dunseverick – a cure on the Causeway Coast of County Antrim.

Here the rectory was beautiful, convenient and friendly. It has the finest views of any rectory in the diocese of Connor.

Let me tell you what I remember of that grand old house, which we all loved very much and were sad to leave when the time came.

Like the Belfast house it was Victorian, but painted bright white, much smaller and utterly picturesque. It still stands on its own little hill flourishing tall chimneys and high pointed gables. The wide bargeboards were cleverly carved to resemble lace collars. The windows and doors are wide and offer a warm welcome to all comers.

The white limestone gravel avenue led straight up from the Lisnagunogue Road. In our day it was resplendent with yellow tails of laburnum, some brushing the lawns. There were banks of bluebells and daffodils in due season. The grounds were surrounded by pine trees – a green arboretum in the north Antrim countryside. This was a rare sight as the area had been deforested by the settlers many years before we came.

You enter into a square hall, to the right is the drawing room and the dining room. Behind the latter is a curious narrow serving pantry. This was a perfect place for us to play *'the shop game'* which we enjoyed. On the other side of the hall my father's study was situated, then the kitchen, scullery and laundry. The lower return landing served the bathroom and the maid's room, where Bessie lived.

Behind the house is the yard and the coach house. It was a grand house for our family, soon to grow to five. There was plenty of water, when we

Dunseverick Rectory.

pumped it up from our deep well. We had soft light by night, when we lit the paraffin oil lamps and candles.

It was several years before my father acquired a motor-car, and only after our old donkey reneged on an important trip to Bushmills. Bushmills was our big town, Coleraine our city. Lisnagunogue village was where most of our daily necessities were satisfied. 'Gonogue or Gunye had one shop, one public house, one street and one church.

The shop rejoiced in the grand title 'The General Store' – and it was very general! It became our sweet shop, when riches accumulated to a penny or two. On such occasions we took a long time to choose between aniseed balls, cinnamon lozenges, pomfret cakes, liquorice and acid drops. This menu we worked through with precision. Vegetables were on sale in season, although most people grew their own supply. We got our lamp oil there; candles, soap, oatmeal for porridge, sewing thread, thick twine, fizzy lemonade, paper and ink.

The shop had a pleasurable odour peculiar to itself. I have never come across that smell anywhere else, but I shall enjoy it till the day I die. Also it was our Post Office, its little wire cage hidden behind a hundred interesting items, which were suspended from the ceiling. In December every year special treats went on display–board games, professionally filled stockings from Father Christmas, a few wooden toys and several fascinating Christmas annuals.

When important guests came to stay at the rectory we got meat for roasting from Bushmills. We had our own chickens for the pot. It was always a tragic time when a favourite hen had to be killed for soup. Our fish came from Port Braddan, Dunseverick Harbour and Ballintoy.

Father was an excellent fisherman and a keen marksman. He would bring home game, shot over Croaghmore Mountain and rabbits from White Park Bay. After visitation of the parishioners, which occupied most afternoons all the year around, he brought back to the rectory gifts of fruit, potatoes, butter, cheese and bacon. Other commodities we grew in the garden or even the house. My mother was an expert with asparagus, which she nursed to life in the spare room. Food was plentiful and delicious, fresh and fragrant, cooked by Bessie on the great black range in the kitchen.

In those days our little kingdom, the rectory glebe, extended towards the cliffs of the Giants Causeway, mostly it was rented annually by local farmers. In the most deserted corner of it there was an old kiln where in days of yore, limestone had been burnt to produce fertiliser for the fields. The kiln had not been used for that purpose for many years, however, it was still in fair repair. Those were the depression years and many men were seeking employment. One James Megaw came to my father requesting the use of the old kiln in which to smoke herrings. He said he was going to sell them to keep body and soul together. Our rather gullible father agreed and the kippering business was established. We benefited by receiving a parcel of kippers every Friday.

Shortly afterwards, one of our favourite kittens fell ill. My young brother Robert, ever a trusting soul, thought that the cure for life was a sip of Communion wine. Alas, none was available. However, we remarked that James Megaw and his helper always had the whiff of the Communion about them. We went up to the kiln to inquire if James would lend us some Communion wine.

There was no-one at home. The door was barred. Robert climbed through a hole in the wall, which appeared to be acting as a chimney. The kiln was full of bottles; we borrowed one of them and carried it back to the rectory.

With great difficulty the sick kitten was introduced to 'Communion wine'. No sooner had we got the elixir of life down the feline throat than it recovered and headed for the garden, at the speed of light.

Looking for praise we reported this miracle cure to our parents. Father was dumbfounded. Off he went to the kiln with his trusty shotgun over his shoulder. All the bottles were thrown over the cliff. The criminal distillers returned, saw the shotgun and fled. I suppose now-a-days I should say *"what a waste of good poteen even though it was distilled*

Lisnagunogue Village shop.

on church land".

The milkman delivered a packet of kippers from Bushmills the following Friday. He said there was no one at the kiln to take Mr Megaw's weekly order – *"would we take it for him?"* *"They will not be back"* said my father and gave the man a shilling.

One day a family of travelling people came to the rectory gates. They lived in a spanking red caravan with a blue roof. A big piebald pony was between the shafts and a little foal clip-clopping along behind, tied to the tail gate.

Neither father nor Bessie were at home. My mother was afraid to open the door. A tall woman with three bare-footed boys came up our avenue. All were romantically featured with brown faces and black hair. In those days we called them gipsies. Today one must call them travelling people. Mother collected us in the drawing room and pulled over the heavy brocade curtains. I was ordered to keep watch from the upstairs windows.

When loud knocks on our front door went unanswered, the woman decided there was no one at home. After surveying the house she went to the yard and catching one of our poor hens, rang its neck, while the boys raided the nests for eggs. Everything was tossed into her skirt, which she gathered up into a useful bag. The laundry washing, which was drying on the line in the garden, joined the plunder in her skirt.

Sadly the loot included a hand-embroidered christening robe. It had been made for me and was required for my little sister Jenny the following Sunday.

When Father came home he set out immediately in hot pursuit, equipped with an apple dumpling, a pot of jam and a farl of soda bread. Soon he returned with the stolen articles. *"Sure all you need to do is to give them something to keep them happy. They have very few of this world's goods"*. All the christening robe required was another good wash to rid it of the smell of smoke and poultry.

Reminiscence of two sad Dunseverick memories are etched on my memory. I was staying with my friend Cathy, who lived on her family's farm at a mile from the rectory. It was harvest time and we were allowed to stay off school in order to help with the in gathering of the crops. The neighbouring farmers helped each other with the hard work.

At the noon-day whistle, Cathy and I carried baskets filled with the harvesters' dinners. We brought fresh soda farls, warm off the griddle, thickly covered with home made butter. There were dozens of hard boiled eggs in their shells and strong sweet tea, ready brewed in silver buttermilk cans.

The workers always cheered when Cathy and I hove into sight. They downed tools, silenced the rattling thresher and stretched out on the warm ground in the sunshine or in the shade of the stooked sheaves. We proffered our baskets. We filled and refilled the blue edged enamel mugs or tins with string handles. Shelled eggs disappeared down hungry throats followed by the soda farls and sweet tea.

Before returning to work some snatched a doze, but the older boys preferred to snatch a lassie, in the hope of a romp behind a rick. My favourite, Willie was only fifteen – too shy to accept the longing looks in his direction. In turn he pick-a-backed Cathy and I around the field, straddling the stooks with ease, until we shrieked with delight.

Then back to work when the dinner hour was over. It was time for Willie to take his turn on the threshing machine. Still flushed with excitement, Cathy and I watched him climb up, strong, brown and handsome.

The clattering machinery came to life. Willie was making sure the sheaves, flying off the forks went neatly into the greedy jaws of the machine. A poke here, there a prod and now a great howl as Willie disappeared.

Shouts, oaths, screams and then silence, as the whirr of the thresher stopped. The driver jumped down into the machinery and lifted Willie's mangled body. When he carried it out a single scream split the silence – and Willie's mother fell to the ground.

Grave stones all over the country testify to the multitude of agricultural accidents to adolescents and the resultant parental sorrow. Few parishioners understand the grief of the one who ministers at the graveside. A more common Grim Reaper in those days was the teen-age illness – tuberculosis.

Mother played the organ in Dunseverick Church, as she had at Blessington. A difficulty was that now at Service time she had Philippa and me on which to keep an eagle eye and little Robert on the organ bench beside her. Near by, Kitty, one of the choir girls, sat directly behind the clergy desk during service.

Kitty often became bored with the prayers and lessons which interspersed the hymns she loved singing full heartily. One Sunday, during the General Confession, Kitty removed the drawing pins from the choir notice board and pinned the hem of my father's snow-white surplus to the top of the choir stall.

When Father stood to pronounce the Absolution, there was a rending and a ripping sound, which resounded around the silent church. Father turned and immediately saw that Kitty was the perpetrator of this unforgivable sin. *"Leave the Church, Kitty"* he ordered quietly. She sat still. He repeated *"Leave the Church"* Kitty looked towards my mother who whispered *"please go like a good girl, Kitty!"*

Dunseverick Church.

So Kitty started on the longest walk of her short life, straight down the centre aisle of Dunseverick parish Church. The former choir girl held her head high, sill defiant, avoiding the scandalised looks of the congregation.

On Monday the rector went to visit Kitty's single parent, who lived on a hillside farm. Kitty refused to speak to him. Father saw her flushed cheeks and the perspiration on her young forehead. He knew she had the dreaded teenage disease of those days – tuberculosis!

My father visited every day, bringing home-made delicacies from the rectory. Kitty always refused to speak. Then one night my father was called to her bedside. Kitty asked for the Confession and the Absolution. *"We have done those things which we ought not to have done; and there is no health in us. He pardoneth all them that truly repent"*. Kitty died the same year. She was only

fifteen years of age. The same age as Willie. In the country, life can be unutterably short and desperately sad.

I could paint you a hundred pictures of life-style during the early years of the last century in the Lisnagonague countryside and around your mill at Port Braddan. How we almost fell over the Giant's Causeway, of Big Hugh and how he conquered the demon drink, how we got to Rathlin Island in those days, of our school master and our doctor. However, some years ago I recorded it all in a book for my grandchildren. I call the book, 'The Children of Dunseverick'. It is out of print now, but you can obtain it in the Bushmills Library, provided you return it within three weeks. It is much in demand. There remain some good friends at Lisnagunogue who remember our days in that peaceful parish. To you all I send my love and very best wishes.

"Tempora mutantur, nos et mutamur in illis.
Vestigia nulla retrorum

138

AUTHOR'S REMARKS

As with "The Letter of a Local Lady" I should not presume to annotate Vivienne Draper's beautifully told story in 'Children of Dunseverick'. Mrs V. Atkinson and Mrs M.A. Young have given us unique eye-witness accounts of Causeway Coast life-style, which few other areas in Ireland possess.

After the Draper family removed from Dunseverick, the Rev. Dr. J.H. Templeton became curate-in-charge of the parish in 1934. Eventually Dunseverick, Ballintoy and Rathlin became a united parish. Today the Dunseverick rectory, in which Vivienne draper spent her happy childhood days, is meticulously maintained by the Denny family. Lisnagunogue means "the fort of the churns."

Tempora mutantur, nos et mutamur in illis. Vestigia nulla retrorum.
"The times are changed and we likewise –
there is no retreat".

The Drumbeg Window

The Drumbeg Door.

XVI A LETTER FROM A GRIEVING MOTHER

LADY CURRAN, PORT BRADDAN 1961 -1968

The only spark of happiness in those anni horribiles, which followed our daughter's murder, was the day our son Michael bought that charming little cottage beside your mill house at Port Braddan.[1] Sir Lancelot and I really enjoyed those few halcyon summers with our grandchildren of whom, perforce, we had seen so little. Michael invited us to come up to the Port Braddan cottage, whenever my husband could get away from the battle of life. He over-crowded every minute with social, political and legal business. Sir Lancelot did this in order to obliterate our mutual mental torture. I preferred to withdraw into our family and pull down the shutters on the whole tragedy.

It was a blast of fresh air to get back to the Causeway Coast, where we had spent so many happy times together during the summer vacations. We enjoyed taking the grandchildren to the hotels which had been our seaside pied-à-terre, when Patricia and her brothers were on vacation from school and university. One good reason why I looked forward to the summer holidays was because it meant I could get away from the depressing house in which we lived during the rest of the year!

Let me tell you about that dark, damp, cold and unloved mansion at Whiteabbey, which Sir Lancelot bought for his growing family and ambition. We went there towards the end of the Second World War. Patricia was only thirteen when we moved to the Glen House. I have always blamed her death on that sad removal. I loathed that house, from the first day. I did my best to placate its evil djinni, during the ten long years which destroyed our family. I was delighted in 1964, when I read in the Belfast Telegraph that it had been burnt to the ground. Would that it has been destroyed by the German bombs which fell on the city in 1941.

The Glen house was designed in the middle of the nineteenth century by the celebrated Belfast architect, Thomas Jackson. He left his *'Helmet'* trade mark on the gate piers. The place was built for the wealthy Pim family, who owned Lisnagarvey House at Lisburn. Lisnagarvey resembled the Glen, in fact the gate lodges were almost identical. Our dire little lodge served the neighbouring mansion, Glenavna, as well as Glen House.

Our house was in the usual style of the Jackson domestic architectural office. It was large, roomy, gloomy and damp. There was an acre of elegant parquetry which had to be kept polished, miles of magnificent stucco to be dusted and a profusion of chocolate brown woodwork, which always required decoration. Of course, it was impossible to heat the house or even to keep it reasonably clean. There was a mile long trail from the kitchens to the dining room, food was always tepid when it reached the table! It was a constant nightmare to entertain Sir Lancelot's many important guests. I am sure some of them thought the house had not seen a decorator's brush since the day the Pim family built it!

To run the house and family, the only 'help' I had was one 'cook-general' as the advertisements called 'housekeepers' in those days. The good woman did her very best, and together we kept

Glen House Gate-lodge

things going. However, we knew only too well that Glen House required an outside and indoor staff to keep it up to a minimal comfort standard. At first I tried, eventually I capitulated to a losing battle!

Today you could not imagine the problem it was to run a home during the war and the years thereafter. When we went to live in Glen House, coal and oil were almost impossible to obtain. In January 1947, the worst winter on record, the meat ration was reduced to twelve pence per week, the following year it was six pence! We got diminutive rations of sugar, butter and bacon. In 1949 the weekly sugar ration was eight ounces and we could buy only four ounces of sweets per week. However things were getting better. Clothes rationing was abolished that same year, but, petrol rationing did not end until May 1950. It was an atrocious time to attempt to give dinner parties, obtain help in the house or bring up a teenage family. If Sir Lancelot was disappointed in my feeble efforts, he never said an unpleasant word or complained about war time restrictions. When Patricia and the boys transgressed, he reprimanded them stringently – sometimes I thought too severely.

Patricia was less than useless round the house and garden. Often I chided that her study bedroom

was a virtual pig-sty and insisted that she would put away her clothes and vacuum the carpets. I told Patricia it was most unfair to expect our housekeeper to wait hand and foot on a teenager. The reply was always the same *'that's the way of the world'* and one of the interminable rows would follow. So I learned to keep my mouth shut.

Sir Lancelot and I thought the children would renovate the original tennis and croquet lawns, which spread before the house. They preferred to play tennis elsewhere, rather than cut the grass. Gradually the gardens became a lush, impassable jungle, devouring the half-mile weed encrusted private avenue, which led to our front door.

All parents expect their children to outlive them. Patricia's early death eclipsed all other events in our lives. Both of us wanted a daughter. Patricia was a beautiful child who made friends with anyone, especially the unnoticed or unwanted children in the playground. She did very well at school and decided to pursue a career in graphic art and design. This was something new to our family, but Sir Lancelot and I did not interfere. Patricia could be most obdurate. We thought that she would marry her steady boyfriend very soon and start an early family.

At school, Patricia was an extremely active member of the Community Service Group and conscientiously visited old and handicapped people, who required help in their little homes in our village. She was good at sport and a very strong girl. I often wondered why she did not put up more of a fight against those who murdered her on November 13, 1952. Our daughter was strong minded, just like Sir Lancelot. Like him, she would turn down the corners of her mouth when thwarted. Then she would look straight through you, like the cruel east wind, which is too mean to blow around you!

Like all pretty little girls, especially those whose peers are male, Patricia loved dressing up in my clothes and experimenting with my cosmetics. I did not encourage such invasions into our bedroom or the immodesty occasioned by such displays in a male household.

On reflection, perhaps I was too severe with my little girl, but then I did not know she was to die at the early age of nineteen years!

Patricia had a continental pen friend, such was all the rage after the war. She had been invited to go over to Europe for a skiing holiday. For some strange reason Sir Lancelot refused to finance the expedition. Patricia took the refusal very badly and retaliated by taking a student-job driving a truck for a local builder. I forget his name, but you can see it painted on lorries and building sites all over the place. Where she obtained a licence to drive a truck I know not, I was teaching her to drive in my own little car! To avoid a blot on the Curran escutcheon I told everyone Patricia had been offered a holiday job as a student chauffeur. However, the job did not last long as one of the work-force made advances towards my beautiful daughter and she ran home to mother! I am sure she gave as good as she received!

Our sons Michael and Desmond were true chips of the Curran block. Their Aunt May of BBC Children's Hour, always remarked this fact when she came to us at Christmas time. After college Michael obtained a lucrative post in Belfast's leading estate agents. He had flown the nest by the time of our catastrophe, but the dust of disapproval descended on all of us. Michael had grandiose notions of building quaint Irish holiday villages, an idea from which others benefited after his premature death. Michael died while still a young father and after the fatal road accident of our dear eldest granddaughter. Two tragedies which further overspilled our cup of grief.

Desmond was completely different to his siblings. He was protective of his parents and

Port Braddan c.1950.

preferred to stay with Sir Lancelot and myself when his brother and sister were enjoying life with their friends. He was concerned with the welfare of other people and solemnly criticised Patricia on the subject of her self indulgence. Even during the school holidays Desmond would prepare for the new term and in his quality time make intricate models, with a skill that we found quite amazing.

It was as if everything Desmond attempted required a perfect conclusion, achieved by the personal targets which he enjoyed setting for himself. Even when he was at Port Braddan he would swim in the freezing water of White Park

Belfast Gaslamp on Vane base

Bay and then spend the rest of the day cycling up and down your impossible local hills. He played rugby with the same dedication. After a brilliant university career Desmond followed his father's footsteps into the legal profession.

I should say I found Desmond's devotion to religion rather frightening. We were a church family, my grandfather had been a clergyman. We were fully connected with the local congregation. Desmond's divine inspiration went far beyond anything Sir Lancelot or I had ever experienced. However, as usual, we kept our opinions to ourselves!

At university Desmond had been interested in the Group Movement. This is an American Society which arrived here at the beginning of the Second World War. Its object is to change peoples lives through honesty, purity, unselfishness and love, by divine guidance. Patricia was unable to appreciate her brother's sincerity. After her murder, Sir Lancelot and I were not surprised when Desmond forsook the legal profession to prepare for the Priesthood. We travelled to Rome for his ordination service. Afterwards he was sent to a missionary parish in Africa. You will remember when we discussed the subject at Port Braddan, I said Desmond decided to award himself a life sentence!.

The fourth member of our family, my husband Sir Lancelot, had a splendid scholastic career with a meteoric rise to the apex of the legal profession. He became a high court judge at forty, Attorney General in 1945 and a Lord Chief Justice of Appeal, shortly after Patricia's murder. Among his many interests he included the Royal Black Preceptory, the Orange Order, the Unionist Party, and the Reform Club. At that time social advance, career and political opportunities came through such associations.

People found him difficult and standoffish. Such qualities were necessary for a judge and came more from innate diffidence, rather than a desire to appear aloof. Upkeep cost of the Glen House, college fees for three clever children, a couple of expensive cars, endless social entertaining and large subscriptions to every organisation in the constituency, required an unlimited annual income.

Sir Lancelot joked with me about Mr Micawber and how we might balance our finances. Neither of us came from wealthy families, which we might approach and I could not go back to work. So Sir Lancelot turned to gambling, cards at the Reform Club and then racehorses with a turf accountant in the village. At first he thought his superior intellect could play and win the field; too late he discovered the thrill compensated for the loss of our money.

Usually it was at the breakfast table that Sir Lancelot made his paternal pronouncements. One morning, shortly before the murder, he pontificated about the necessity of economy and security. Patricia's allowance was to be restricted. The Glen House was to be sold. Personal keys were to be kept under surveillance. I was accustomed to such legal verbiage and allowed it to wash over me without comment, but Patricia took it all very badly. For some unfathomable reason she liked the Glen House; I could not wait to get away from it! After Patricia's murder the media exaggerated my husband's peccadilloes, in order to heighten sensation value.

I am sure you remember meeting Sir Lancelot at Port Braddan and the conversations you had sitting in the sun in the front garden of our lovely little cottage[1]. He enjoyed those relaxing holidays in that idyllic place, beside the Sea of Moyle.

Now let me tell you what happened on that horrible night which eclipsed our family lifestyle for ever. It was November 13, 1952. I spent the afternoon shopping in Belfast at the Robinson and Clever city centre store. Christmas was five weeks ahead and I was looking for suitable presents for the family.

The thirteenth turned out to be a beastly November day – cold and wet! I got home about six o'clock and immediately put into the oven our evening meal, which my housekeeper had prepared. Sir Lancelot and Desmond came home in good time for dinner but Patricia did not appear at table. This was not unusual. Indeed, that very morning we shared angry words over her late arrivals. The previous evening she had returned home in an unfamiliar car, which

Botanic Gardens Gatehouse with weathervane. Watercolour. 25 x 18cms.

parked on our drive for a long time. I thought her absence from dinner was an attempt to punish me for the breakfast time quarrel. Also because we had forbidden her to smoke in the dining room.

When Patricia had not returned from college by one o'clock in the morning we became very worried. At one forty-five, Sir Lancelot telephoned her current boyfriend. I repeat the time of that call was one forty-five because the boy said he had received the call after two o'clock! He told Sir Lancelot that they had intended to play squash after lectures. Unfortunately, he had forgotten to reserve a court, so they were unable to get a game. They went for coffee and afterwards Patricia had boarded the Whiteabbey local bus, at five o'clock. Later it was claimed that the clock on the terminus building was slow by ten minutes.

A half-hour later at five thirty, the conductor assisted Patricia to get off his bus at our gates[2]. Patricia required his help because she was carrying her squash racket, books, a large art folio and an umbrella. When we received the news from Patricia's boyfriend, we became extremely agitated. My husband immediately telephoned to the local police station and to his friend, our solicitor. I telephoned the police station again, to inquire if any news had come to light, but Sir Lancelot cancelled the call, saying they would need all the time we can give them to work on the case. Then he and Desmond hurried out into the pelting rain to search our avenue.

Often we worried about Patricia's necessary night walks from the Shore Road to the Glen House. When possible, someone would go to meet her at the gates. Sadly no one had done so on that wet November night.

Sir Lancelot told me our local policeman had cycled up about two o'clock. While the search was in progress, suddenly there came a loud cry from Desmond. He had found Patricia. Her poor body was lying about ten yards from the avenue, in the dead leaf-sodden shrubbery. Patricia's scarf was nearby and her right-hand glove lay a couple of yards from the prostrate body. Desmond lifted his sister and declared she was still breathing. Tragically it was only air expelling from the corpse.

Later that morning, nearer the avenue, they found Patricia's books, art folder, handbag and hat. Strangely she was carrying an unposted letter to her pen friend[3]. Apparently this was the last thing she had written and had forgotten to post the letter. The squash racket and umbrella were never found.

Desmond and our solicitor placed Patricia's stiffening body unto the back seat of the car. This presented great difficulty as the arm on which she had been lying was elevated and stiff. They rushed to the surgery in the hope that our doctor could revive my poor daughter. Still half asleep, the doctor examined the body and said Patricia had been shot! He estimated she had been dead for over four hours, but said the exact time would be determined at the autopsy. Then it was discovered that the wounds on my child's body were thirty-seven thrusts by a sharp knife.

The constable cycled back to the police station to report the murder to his Inspector, who immediately informed the Chief Inspector of the Royal Ulster Constabulary. Meanwhile, my husband hurried back to our house to tell me about the tragedy. We embraced and offered meaningless words with which we comforted each other. Then Sir Lancelot set about the gruesome duty of informing the family, before the catastrophe would become public knowledge in the newspapers.

The three days between that horrific night and Patricia's funeral are a blank sheet to me. The doctor and a few members of our family were admitted to my bedroom. Desmond saw to all the interment arrangements and our faithful housekeeper tended to our every need. The funeral service was held in the drawing room. The large room was filled with Sir Lancelot's colleagues and our relatives. A huge crowd of Patricia's friends and local people gathered on the ill-kept driveway in front of the house. Women do not attend funeral processions in Ireland. From the drawing room window I watched the slow cortege move down the avenue. At the gate lodge my daughter's coffin was put into the hearse for the slow procession to the graveyard.

The following weeks were abhorrent. I ate, slept and raged in my room. The doctor came every day with pills and potions, which I did not want to consume. Sir Lancelot kept me informed of events, which I did not want to hear.

They cleared everything from Patricia's room and removed all the mementoes of her which were scattered around the house. When I came out of my trance, it was as if she had never lived in Glen House. That was the first time I realised my daughter was dead. I broke down completely and wept for hours, which relief I had been unable to obtain previously.

I learned that while I had been in absentia, the police had requested permission to search the house, in case Patricia's murderer had been an escaping burglar. Of course, Sir Lancelot told them that nothing was missing and as our daughter had not returned home on that November night, there was no reason why I should be disturbed unnecessarily by a house search.

During the following weeks a special incident room was set up in the village. It seemed as if the world media were present in the Glen day and night. I seldom went outside and we kept all the blinds and curtains tightly closed. Of course, Sir Lancelot and Desmond had to go about their business as usual; but they were most considerate that my wishes to be left alone were enforced.

The days dragged on without a successful discovery of the assassin. Local police detectives were replaced with experts from Scotland Yard in England.[4] I read the day by day accounts of the investigations in the local and national press. The reports seldom agreed and the sensational headlines appeared to describe an event taking place in a foreign country.

Perhaps that is why the Chief Constable thought the culprit was one of the overseas service men who were billeted in the village and still awaiting repatriation. Many were questioned, none was charged. From that group it was only a step to suspect the Royal Air Force personnel who were stationed in the area. All of them were questioned, only one came under intensive police scrutiny.

Iain Hay Gordon was one of Desmond's many friends, with whom he hoped to share the ideas of the Group Movement. The young Scotsman was an accounts clerk at the local airforce base. I suppose he was lonely, being single and far away from home. Desmond invited him to come to the Glen House. We always encouraged our family to invite their friends to enjoy our home.

The day Iain Gordon chose to call, Desmond was not at home. Patricia received him warmly, as she always did, and entertained him in the drawing room until Desmond returned from court. A couple of weeks before the murder, Desmond invited the young man to come for Sunday luncheon. Patricia brought him into the drawing room where we were sitting, after church attendance. Desmond introduced him to us. Sir Lancelot glanced over his glasses, nodded and continued to read the Sunday papers.

I saw a shy young Scottish airman, spick, span and polished up for the occasion. He desperately desired to please his hosts but was completely tongue tied. My heart went out to him! Before Sunday luncheon our family custom was to say Grace, our hands joined with each other. This little pleasantry seemed to embarrass our guest, and from there it was downhill all the way!

Patricia was coy towards the airman and arch to her father in order to attract the young man's attention. Desmond chided her and the rest of the meal was eaten in complete silence. I am sure Iain Hay Gordon was glad to escape from Glen House, never to return!

Without a doubt, Gordon's arrest was due to his visits to the Glen. The fact that he knew Patricia personally and had attended her funeral, attracted special police suspicion.

Photographs of the poor young man started to appear in the newspapers, after he had been taken for questioning. Then it was reported that he had concocted an alibi for the time of the murder. Crime journalists alleged that the Scotland Yard officers had procured a confession, which the suspect airman had signed. Desmond's friend went on trial for the murder of my daughter Patricia.

Consideration was given to the possible inadmissibility of Gordon's confession. However, the judge decided the police had acted properly. The jury brought in a negative verdict and cited insanity.[5] Iain was sentenced to be detained in a secure mental institution at Her Majesty's pleasure.

The purgatory in which we have lived ever since replaced the four months of hell. Desmond went off to Africa, Michael had his own family. Patricia was dead. Sir Lancelot and I are left together to discover a way in which to live with our tragedy.

So now you know why it is such a joy to get up to Port Braddan and enjoy a happy family visit with our grandchildren.

Sometimes I go into your tiny church to sit listening for the waves washing on the sandy beach and the happy cries of children playing with their siblings. Sometimes I think about the story of Saint Gobban's shadow of blessing and forgiveness. Always I remember my beautiful daughter Patricia and wonder why God allows such horrible things to happen. But life must go on for those of us who are left.

Che Sara Sara.[6]

Belfast weathervane

147

AUTHOR'S NOTES

Iain Hay Gordon commenced his detention on March 6, 1953. Although the jury brought in a verdict of insanity, Gordon did not receive psychotherapy during his years in prison. Authorities did not consider mental health treatment necessary. On December 20, 2000, an appeal court held that the confession which Gordon had made for the murder of Patricia Curran was inadmissible. The verdict was overturned and the appeal was allowed.

At least four points remain unanswered.

(a)   Patricia's squash racket and umbrella were never found.
(b)   The R.A.F. did not supply 'official issue knives'. A knife discovered beyond Carrickfergus on the Belfast Lough Shore had no proven connection with the case.
(c)   Iain Hay Gordon did not receive the R.A.F. Officer assistance, which is required to be given to service men.
(d)   Patricia Curran's killer was never found.

1.   The Currans bought Rossneath Cottage from Mrs Anderson in 1960. Its large living room had once been the dining room of John McKay's guest house. Accommodation included two bedrooms, a kitchen and a bathroom. Probably the cottage was the original building in Port Braddan village. Its rafters were acquired from a shipwreck at Gid Point, its walls were Causeway and rubble stones and its floors were quarry tiled. The cottage was tumbled in 1999 and replaced by a modern balconied house.

2.   In 1952 public service omnibuses were served by both drivers and conductors. The latter received fares and looked after the safety and comfort of passengers.

3.   It seems this was the girlfriend who had invited Patricia to come to the continent for a skiing holiday.

4.   It was most unusual for R.U.C. detectives to be replaced by Scotland Yard Crime Investigators in an ordinary inquiry.

5.   Capital punishment was awarded for murder in 1952. A verdict of insanity avoided the hanging of the guilty party.

6.   (Italian) What will be, will be.

XVII A LETTER FROM A GOOD NEIGHBOUR,

MARJORIE KIRKPATRICK. PORT BRADDAN 1960 – 1994

First of all, let me thank you for the invitation to pen a few words to your mill house for inclusion in a collection of essays. I have plenty of time to do so here in Ballycastle Hospital. We have been good neighbours for almost forty years and shared our industry, sociability and interest in Port Braddan.

Born with a name like Kirkpatrick, I was bound to be Irish, at least from my fathers kith and kin. The Kirkpatricks are descended from George, who came to Ireland in 1690 as an officer in King William's army. One of our relatives was the Empress Eugenie, consort of Napoleon III. I shall never forget my impressions of that unfortunate lady on the day my father took me to meet her. The Empress ended up at Farnborough, where she died in 1920, when I was a little girl of eleven years of age. For many years I kept Eugenie's framed bridal veil on the wall of the drawing room at Rossneath House.[1]

My father returned to England to avoid the troubled times, when the twenty-six southern counties seceded from the United Kingdom. My younger sister Daphne and I have many relatives in Dublin with whom we have corresponded and visited over the years. So, being at least half Irish, I assumed there would be no difficulty in returning to the north coast, as a summer person, with the intention of making Port Braddan my locale when teaching days were over.[2] Assumptions can be dangerously inaccurate. However, I found my belief to be commonly and delightfully correct, that the Causeway Coast is the most beautiful part of the Irish landscape.

Perhaps that which others consider in me as aloofness or superiority comes from innate shyness, self-sufficiency and an early nurture in India. I was not a healthy child, I almost died at birth. My little sister more than compensated by rotund robustness, which developed my need to paddle my own canoe! Daphne was our memsahib's darling, even though my dear parents always advocated fair play.

My father was Dr. Henry Kirkpatrick, Colonel in the Indian Medical Service. He was in charge of the government Ophthalmic Hospital and professor of the Medical College in Madras. A special field of study was cataract and its treatment. His book of that title shows his expertise in ophthalmic operations, which is his contribution to India and humanity in general.[3]

As my father was a British army officer and chief medical officer in Madras, our position in India was highly superior. My mother had a staff of servants to run the bungalow; maids did the housework, boys tended the beautiful gardens and young men, wearing white gloves, served at table. In the nursery our memsahib, with a couple of maids, looked after Daphne and myself.

This was a privileged childhood indeed, and one that instilled in me a deep respect for those who serve and a full understanding why the British Raj came to an end on August 15, 1947. By that time we had returned home to Sandy Rise at Yateley in Surrey, a beautiful neo-tudor country house with a magnificent garden. It was at Sandy Rise that I learned the considerable horticultural skills which have enriched my life ever since. While I gardened my sister learned equestrianism, which took her to the highest amateur eminence of that proficiency.

I went up to Cambridge to read Modern Languages with Spanish as my forte. I gained a First without any difficulty. I was always as fond of French and Spanish as I had been of Hindi, which my sister and parents found so difficult. What I discovered hard to understand was why a woman student could not have her Cambridge University degree conferred at Commencements! Even so, I remained a member of the University Women's Association and always used the club's accommodation when I was in London.

My first teaching post was at Jersey Ladies College. Here I made many friends and not a few adversaries among my colleagues and students. In Jersey I met John and Mary Grummitt. John was Headmaster of the equally prestigious Victoria College on the island. Later he became Principal of your Royal Belfast Academical Institution. We had to evacuate the island when the Germans invaded on July 1, 1940. The Grummitts went to Ireland, I came home to Sandy Rise. Soon I was travelling over to the Emerald Isle for holidays; Ireland was the only place one could go in wartime Europe! It was then that I decided to buy an Irish property. I spent many summer vacations searching for *'the right place'*.

In 1960 I bought Rossneath House, a farmstead and former guest house at Port Braddan on the coastal path of the Ulster Way. The owners, my good friends John and Martha McKay, removed to their second house on the cliff top. Here John continued to farm the surrounding area, until the McCurdy family acquired the lands. I had much in

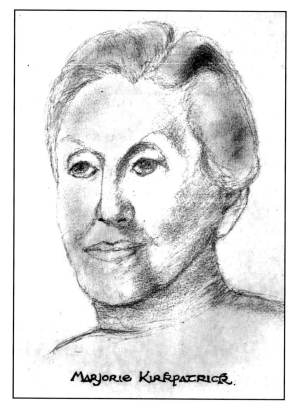

MARJORIE KIRKPATRICK.

common with John McKay, who possessed a scientific knowledge of the area and a unique ability to train sheepdogs.

What attracted me to the McKay family farmhouse was the possibility of cultivating a splendid sheltered garden by the seaside. The unending miles for hiking expeditions around the Giant's Causeway and White Park Bay[1] were a big attraction. The southern outlook on a north coast[2] is a unique position for special horticulture. What clenched the deal was the odd little window set out of line, which admits a sea view to the upstairs landing of Rossneath House.

Rossneath is a traditional Ulster farm house,

four square three bay and two dormers. When Martha ran the boarding house she had ten bedrooms and thirty guests demanding attention every summer season.[3] This she did with complete satisfaction; forty years later tourists still arrive looking for accommodation! When I bought the house there were four bedrooms and two reception rooms. Previously the adjoining garage had provided two bedrooms. On the south side of the house there was an older building, possibly the original eighteenth century stedding. It is marked on the first Ordnance Survey maps. In that old cottage there had been the guests' dining room and four additional bedrooms.

The old wing of the boarding house was converted into a cottage and sold to Mrs Anderson, who became a valued friend. Like myself she loved Port Braddan. One afternoon when we were gathering fruit in the garden she requested that when she died, after cremation her ashes would be scattered on my sea garden. Mrs Anderson spent her days walking on the sands and sitting in the sea garden, reading her best loved books. Of course, I was only too happy that she would be laid to rest in my garden at Port Braddan.[4]

Beyond Mrs Anderson's cosy cottage lay what became your farmyard and the old mill building, in which John and Martha lived during the tourist season.

The great day came when I brought a few pieces from Sandy Rise to Rossneath and set up house. Then with Molly Harrison, my dear friend and teaching colleague, we acquired furniture at an antique shop in Ballycastle and from local auction sales all over the countryside. I brought home wooden chairs from our annual Spanish escapades, which artist Molly painted in the traditional Iberian style. Later, when I retired and took up permanent

Port Braddan from the harbour. c1950.

151

residence, I brought over to Ireland a grand collection of English antique furniture and object d'art.

For most of the removals I used my trusty camper van. I like to think I invented campervaning in the 1950's. I ordered a special Bedford van chassis and engaged a carpenter to construct a caravan thereon.[5] It had living accommodation for five adults, cooking and heating equipment, fold-away bunks and tables, and an extension canvas awning, for sitting under on sunny days. Even my love for Port Braddan could not make me forsake the annual pilgrimage to Spain and France. Of course, I used the journeys to carry back curiosities for Rossneath House.

Port Braddan Millhouse.

Various facilities had to be added to the house; usually these were undertaken during the winter months when Molly and I were teaching in England. Always it was a great excitement to discover the results when we came over to Ireland for the long vacation. Reliable electric space and water heating was added. The lovely old Aga cooker was replaced with a handmade brick fireplace. This vandalism was necessary because the Aga tended to rust when seldom used, in the winter season. Soon a new rear passage, which Molly called *"The Slipe"* afforded interior entry to the garage. The scullery was renovated, a downstairs lavatory and a new upstairs bathroom appeared. Soon the house was comfortable and always welcoming when we came through the front door.

When all these renovations were completed, I decided to offer the house for rent during the summer season to parties of students, while we were on the continent collecting items of interest for Rossneath. I found these "lettings" unsatisfactory, unproductive unnecessary and troublesome.

Our next project, perhaps the primary object, was the gardens. My property surrounded my neighbour's house on three sides, giving me the large cliff sheltered rear garden. It was this that had induced me to acquire Rossneath House in the first place. Towards the sea it gave me the land and roadway in front of my neighbours house. I exchanged this area for the part of my sea garden which was in front of Mrs Anderson's cottage. This little bit of land exchange caused the padlocking of the path along which I dragged my wheeled bin for collection. Of course, this occasioned words which, on reflection, would have been better left unspoken!

After I retired to live permanently at Port Braddan, the gardens became my daily pleasure activity. The horticultural foundations had been laid in the 1960's. Charlie Lynch, who lived with his family in Ballintoy, was the artificer who created from my meticulous paper plans, the Spanish paths and vegetable beds raised on Causeway stones. These stones, which Charlie threw around like pebbles (he had been a British solider) came from the quarry on the Mosside Road. The tiles for the paths were carefully chosen in Spain and brought home in the campervan. The many tons of concrete which the projects devoured, were mixed by hand.[6]

Every time I returned from England the van, like the ship of an early garden plant collector returning from the new world, was filled with rare species for Port Braddan. Thousands of spring bulbs were set out under the trees. Collections of special shrubs and plants were carefully positioned. Raspberries, gooseberries, loganberries and currants took kindly to the mild seaside climate. The vegetables, which were set out in the early spring, never failed to produce a bumper harvest.

You will remember how Charlie and your good self built the sea wall to protect our new sea garden. It was then, with the help of your students that we created another magic demesne. It took place with considerable difficulty as winter waves devoured the previous summer's work. Without Charlie Lynch and Matthew McNeill, I could not have created one of the finest gardens on the north coast. As housework is my bete noire, I should have been unable to spend every day in my garden without the indoor help of Mabel Rodgers and Rose McKay.

Shortly after I came to Port Braddan my attention was called to a solution for the *"Ulster Troubles"* – as they euphemistically called them.

Through Community Service Volunteers, I threw open the door of Rossneath House to followers of both Ulster traditions. With your help we entertained Belfast families from the Shankill and the Falls roads. I hoped that a week away from the source of agitation in the summer sunshine of beautiful White Park Bay, would help the peace effort. Community volunteers sent us problem families, lonely senior citizens like myself, difficult children and convalescents. Sometimes our guests spilled over into your cottage.[7]

If the project was successful I know not – it was not universally welcome, as some observers thought political antagonists would have been better staying in Belfast city!

One thing I was unable to understand about the Irish was the blank acceptance of street litter and effluence of waste into the sea. Molly and I kept a Pig Book. When we saw tourists drop rubbish, we invited them to sign our Port Braddan visitors' book. When they had written their names in the book, we turned it over to show the photograph of a pig on the back cover! Before we came to Rossneath House, Moyle Council did not collect domestic refuse. We bagged our rubbish and delivered it to the Council Offices in Ballycastle. Soon a weekly collection commenced!

Looking back, I suppose some of my English ways did not endear me to all my neighbours. But I did have the full support of the National Trust. In response, I determined that Port Braddan should become a National Trust village, similar to Kearney on the Ards Peninsula of County Down.[8]

As you know, you and I agreed to bequeath our properties and sea-board lands to the National Trust on condition that the other three cottages in the little hamlet would be acquired when they came unto the market. Previously my testamentary intention had been to bequeath Rossneath to the Gardners' Benevolent Trust. I hoped a retired horticulturist would continue to get pleasure from the gardens as I have done over the years. However, the National Trust assured me that the house would be available for the Warden of the Causeway Coast, the gardens would be in safe keeping and the village preserved for posterity.[9]

I had looked forward to the fulfilment of these plans and to the enjoyment of Port Braddan for many years ahead. However, as Boswell says, *"Hell is paved with good intentions"*. In 1990 I started to experience little lapses of consciousness. I received a fall when I was collecting fertiliser from the Port Braddan cave[10], as I was working in my beloved garden. A minor skirmish with a tractor, when I was driving the car, put an end to a long motoring career.

It would have been impossible for me to exist at Port Braddan without a motor car. I had to get into Bushmills for stores and to Ballintoy church for communion. My friends required regular attention and it was essential to get to Coleraine to visit the area culture centre at the University of Ulster.

Regretfully, at my sister's order, I negotiated the purchase of a sheltered accommodation unit at Yately. While clearing Rossneath House for the removal to England, I had another little lapse of consciousness. So here I am in Ballycastle Hospital. The antiques and art effects I shall take to Yately are in storage at the Causeway. The remainder of the furniture is for the use of the National Trust warden and there are mementoes for all my many friends.

Everyone in the hospital has shown great kindness and all my friends have visited me in this special ward. Of course these are return visits – for I was ever a great visitor of other perople!

I hope to be out of hospital next week. Come again soon and please bring with you a large bunch of sunshine yellow primroses from the Rossneath garden.

Best wishes as ever.

"Ars est celare artem."[11]

The Dunville Bell

AUTHORS NOTES

Miss Marjorie Kirkpatrick did not return to England. She died in Ballycastle Hospital on April 12, 1994. At the memorial service in Ballintoy Parish Church the large bouquet of Port Braddan primroses, which she had requested, became a wreath to cover the coffin. After cremation Marjorie's ashes were interred in the family grave, with her father and mother, at Yateley in England. Some of her many friends met together for a memorial service in St. Gobban's Church.

1.   Empress Eugenie (1826-1920) daughter of a Spanish Grandee settled in Paris, where she met and married the future Emperor of France, Napoleon III. During the war of Italian Liberation (1850) she acted as Regent. After the Franco-Prussian war (1870) Eugenie fled to Farnborough in England. Eugenie died during a visit to Spain in 1920, at the advanced age of 94.

2.   Neither Marjorie nor Daphne married. Marjorie taught modern languages in various schools, specializing in Spanish

3.   Henry Kirkpatrick Indian Medical Service, Professor Madras Medical College and Superintendent of the Madras Ophthalmic Hospital. Author of 'Cataract and its Treatment'. (London 1921). Marjorie and Daphne created 'The Kirkpatrick Scholarship' to their father's memory in 1996. The scholarship's valve is £16,500 per annum for post graduate research at the London School of Hygiene and Tropical Medicine.

4.   After prayers in St. Gobban's Church, Mrs Anderson's ashes were scattered on the lower patio, where she was accustomed to make herself comfortable on sunny afternoons. Unfortunately, the Planning Authority permitted the erection of a sceptic tank on the site.

5.   Marjorie claimed that her *"Campervan"* was the first example to roam the roads of the United Kingdom. I am unable to confirm this belief, but I can establish no earlier date! The van ended its useful days with the Community Service Group of the Royal Belfast Academical Institution.

6.   Marjorie created a series of easily maintained paths and patios, which were attractively decorated with Spanish tiles, decorative bricks and finials. These emphasised the colours of the collections of rare plants.

7.   The *"Visitor's Book"* records a long list of city dwellers of all ages and every political opinion. Marjorie was an excellent cook; her guests were given free accommodation. The hope was that a holiday away from all sectarian strife would win support for the Peace Movement, when our guests returned to Belfast.

8. When the remaining three houses at Port Braddan came unto the property market, the National Trust did not acquire them.

9. As yet Rossneath House has not become the residence of the National Trust Warden for the Causeway Coast and the gardens have become a wilderness.

10. See *"The Archaeologists Letter"*. During the later years of the 20th Century the cave was used by cattle for shelter from the Atlantic storms. Marjorie transported many tons of fertiliser from the cave for her garden.

11. The essence of Art is to conceal the Artistry.

The Barque Galathea.

Galathea was built by A & F Smith at Tvedestrand, Norway in 1853; she was wrecked on the bar at Yougal, Co. Cork, in 1858 carrying 630 tons of Guano from Callao, Peru to Cowes in England. Movements before wreckage were: 14th July, 1857, arrived Callao from Montevideo, Uruguay, sailed for Chincha, Peru on 22nd August; 17th October arrived back at Callao and departed on the return voyage for Europe on 22nd October 1857. Lloyds list for 8th February records: Youghal, Galathea went ashore on this bar today during a heavy SSE gale and has healed over broadside to the sea. Crew saved. 11th February Galathea has become a total wreck; none of the cargo saved. 13th February: Galathea broke up on night of 8th, the next morning the strand for a mile was strewn with it. Yesterday the wreck was sold. The Cork Examiner records that a local pilot tried to board Galathea to take her into Cork harbour but his craft could not catch her. Watched by 2,000 spectators the lifeboat rescued the 16 crew who clambered over the bowsprit. Life Boat for 1st July 1858 records that the captain had mistaken Youghal for Queenstown in the south gale and heavy seas. In 1857 the RNLI had supplied the new Peake life-boat for Youghal. (30 ft. 10 oars and 14 crew.) She had a hard pull for two miles against the tide and wind but rescued the distressed crew two hours before Galathea became a total wreck. The ship's bell is preserved at 'The Braddan' Port Braddan, Bushmills.

From 1840 Peru exported guano to Europe. In days prior to artificial fertilizers it provided all the constituents of readily assimilated plant food. Guano is the excrement of certain sea-fowl with other animal remains such as feathers and bones and was found in great abundance on the Chinchas Islands off the coast of Peru. Import to Europe amassed great fortunes for traders and ships' captains and made the voyage around Cape Horn worthwhile.

The Galathea Bell

XVIII   A LETTER FROM THE MILL HOUSE, FROM 1962 INTO THE NEW MILLENNIUM – CON AULD

For the sake of political correctness, that unfortunate proclivity of the present century, I write this letter to a hypothetical miller, as every mill must have its operator. You will see my employment had little to do with the grinding of corn!

The first time I saw Port Braddan, the tiny hamlet was emerging from the summer sea mists which float across White Park Bay in the early morning sunshine.

The haze heralded a fine north Antrim morning and we had much to do and see. The previous day, I had cycled around Lanyon's famous coast road with a couple of examination freed school friends. We crawled into White Park Youth Hotel in the evening dusk, tired, stiff and starving. We had booked *"an overnight"* in the old army hut which replaced the little whitewashed cottage by the strand. Since then the hostel has been replaced twice, first by a rather elegant building and then by the imitation of a first grade hotel, which present day political correctness requires!

That particular morning, over a half century ago, the Port Braddan clachan of sea level cottages was reflected in a shimmering mirage on the green gold waters of the Causeway Coast. The bewitching picture has rejoiced my memory with a special invitation ever since. However, that day we were engaged to visit a giant, sail the Portrush funship and get to Stradreagh Hostel for the night.

The dream endured. College days speeded past. After voyages to the States and Australia I came home to God's own country. As soon as possible I set out on my first motor scooter to find a cottage by the sea. Memory led me back to White Park, to the new hostel which retained the long remembered view. This time Port Braddan was mantled with a

Port Braddan Millhouse.

rare cloak of snow. It was a magic place, a magnet for a hungry cottage hunter. The January morning revealed a snow-bound countryside. Rathlin Island was a white finger pointing towards Port Braddan. The horizon was fringed by Scotland, scintillating in the winter sunshine.

With some difficulty I slid and skidded the scooter down the vee bends into Port Braddan. By a fortunate chance I found that the brayfoot properties of John McKay were for sale. John and Martha had removed to *"Four Winds"* on the cliff top to run their Templastragh farm on level land. Rossneath House and cottage had been sold already; the remaining buildings were available for purchase. It was one of those exceptionable chances in life, when you arrive at the right place at the right time. An opportunity which if missed is regretted for the remainder of your days.

I completed the transaction at the asking price and took possession of *"The Braddan"* during the following month of May. It became the best purchase I have made and has provided interest and industry down the years. There can be no greater pleasure than designing and recreating your own house from an old building, which holds the history of previous centuries within its walls.

From the outset I decided that I should do the actual physical work and all the design technique with my own hands. Accordingly, I prepared ground plans and elevation drawings for the planning committee of the former Antrim County Council. In those days, a decade before local government was reorganised, planning permission was a very serious matter for the authorities. This was especially true for applications in coastal areas. Quite unlike today when, even in areas of special natural beauty, any aggressive developer with preferential connections, has carte blanche!

In 1962 I was forbidden to alter the exterior appearance of the three stone agricultural buildings I had acquired from John McKay. Of course, I had neither intention nor ambition so to do! In places the walls are almost three feet thick, built from sea washed and local stone. Some of the roof rafters come from a ship which was wrecked off the nearby Gid Point.

Let me tell you what I had acquired for conversion into a dwelling house. There was the coach house which adjoined the former boarding house and had served as a garage for the guests. Behind the coach house, at a few feet higher into the cliff stood the mill. At that time it was being used as a stable and a byre. Upstairs in the mill was a storage floor, where John and Martha kept a temporary bedroom. They slept there when

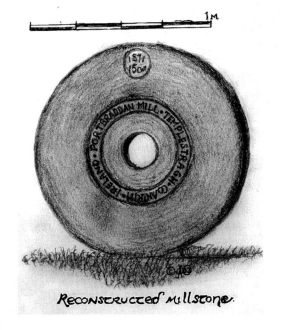

Reconstructed millstone.

Rossneath guest house was filled with visitors. The third building was a little calf house, beautifully constructed with an angled door case and roofed with huge Bangor blue slates. Eventually it became St. Gobban's Church.

Antrim County Council accepted my plans without requiring alteration and I was in business! The most pressing necessity was to provide space for habitation in the coach-house while the property was being converted into a cottage.

Three basics were necessary – Water, Light and Heat. Paraffin oil provided light and heat; a Primus cooker prepared meals fit for kings to devour at the end of work-weary days. The original water supply was captured in two oak barrels which were given

Titanic sidelight

to me by the famous Bushmills distillery. Our drinking water was collected from a little spring on the shore opposite the cottage.

For many years John McKay had been walking over the property with a divining rod, to find a second well to supply his thirsty boarding house. A decade later I came upon a quarry, long hidden under layers of brambles, where he had been excavating for water. It seems, one day when he was chiselling into the cliff face, Martha summoned him for mid-day dinner. When John returned, replete with his wife's good food, he found several tons of rock had fallen on the actual spot where he had been striking the cold chisel into the cliff! Certain death averted, John never returned to the site. I found the chisel still in place, when the brambles were cut out root and branch!

Engineer McKay then turned his talents from divining water to diverting the Templastragh burn over the cliff into Portacallan. Into the new water channel he constructed a little reservoir, from which he laid a pipe to the guest house over the area which later became my garden.

John McKay was one of those inventive pioneers who could produce utilities from ingenuity. The private reservoir served Rossneath House until mains water arrived at Port Braddan in 1964. The project had a second intention. A water fall of some fifty feet now cascaded down the Portacallan cliff. John McKay intended to drive a hydro-electric plant from the waterfall. Another clever project was a cable trolley for easy transport of heavy laden milk cans from the cow pastures at the top of the cliffs to the farmyard at sea level. I found the rusting machinery hidden under brambles when I got around to constructing the garden.

I had greater success in divining for water. I

dug a deep hole in line with McKay excavations. Immediately it filled with water. Perhaps the rock fall which almost killed John McKay, liberated an underground spring. My well has remained full of water ever since. As it was above the level of the cottage, gravity fed our needs. Eventually a Victorian pump was erected for use in the garden.[1] Soon public service electricity and a mains water supply came to the village. However, I still treasure the golden lamp light and sweet springwell water of those early days.

Two dominant ideas determined the interior design of the cottage – uninterrupted space and a nautical theme, always conditioned by the view from the windows. The first idea was achieved by replacing halls and corridors with januaries.[2] The sea scope was obtained by suitable furnishing and the vista.

I converted the coach-house into a large living room with temporary cooking facilities, a ship's sleeping cabin, a platform for the grand piano and a lavatory. Sewage did not present a planning problem as John McKay had provided an efficient septic tank on the property. It was interesting to discover that the septic tank was built within the tail-race which had served the former water mill.[3] Someone in a previous century had constructed a stone walled tunnel running down to the sea which now was completely concealed by the beach. It is covered by flat rectangular cut stones, in size one foot by three feet and four inches in thickness. These were so expertly cut and closely fitted that I found it impossible to reinsert the final slab. It became a seat supported by a

couple of Causeway stones; you will find it in front of the church door. Rest and be thankful!

Now let us return to the interior and lower cottage. As a special feature, I retained the original unplastered party wall. It contains many fine Causeway stones. The other walls were decked with wooden panels given to me by the owner of Beaconfield House on Kensington Road in Belfast. The corner cabinet was part of her kind gift to the cottage.[4] For a chandelier, I converted the ship's wheel from a sailing clipper which my seafaring father acquired during his travels. The compass binnacle in the mill house comes from the same source. Perhaps the most interesting piece in the downstairs sitting room is a Titanic deck-chair. When 'Titanic' sailed from the Harland and Wolff shipyard, many items were left behind in Belfast, presumably retained for shipment when she returned from the maiden voyage. The most important piece is the captain's chart table which now resides in the Belfast harbour master's office. Titanic did not return to Ireland. When her side plates were

Titanic deckchair.

ruptured by an iceberg she sank in the Atlantic ocean, after four days service!

Ships built at Belfast had a reserve equipment store in the shipyards. In 1962 the storekeeper told me I was very fortunate to acquire five sidelights from the Titanic store. He joked *"the firm does not need them any longer"*. Of course, all that was in the middle of the last century. Titanic had not achieved the aura of fame which she has acquired since then.

It was fortunate that my parents had built a retirement place in the 'Martello' orchard. This lucky event produced a surplus collection of family furniture, which would not fit into their new bungalow. It was just the ticket for my cottage! The sitting room inherited a large bookcase and a chaise longue which had been crafted for *'Jocelyn Cottage'*[5] A Wellington chest came from Rossneath, a couple of teak chairs from India,[6] and collection of model yachts.[7]

All this gave us conformable but rather limited accommodation. The next step was to connect the coach house with the old mill. Formerly the pathway into the farm-yard divided the two buildings. This area affords lots of space for a garden room. It is entered through the front door, opposite which is a glass door opening into the garden. A short staircase leads down to the sitting room and two additional cabins. The four rooms are approached through a january, which provides a convenient corner for an eighteenth century cupboard.

The cabins are furnished with the bunks and toilet chiffonier from cabin number 13 of *"RMS Pretoria Castle"*[8]

In the garden room I found space for a dug-out canoe, apparently dating back to the days of Saint Patrick[9]. Above the entrance into the Mill Room I put a curtain pediment of the seventeenth century.[10] In the windows I set a collection of Irish and American glass floats, originally used to carry fishing nets.[11]

So it was in the early 1970's that work commenced on the old mill itself. The floors presented the first problem. The antique structure had been built on two levels, to accommodate the cliff foundations. Each level had been used for stabling or stalling animals in recent years. Before converting such accommodation for human use, the floor must be removed in its entirety. If you omit this chore, the odour of urinary ammonia will permeate the air when the replacement room is heated! All the old cobble-stones had to be removed and the floors replaced with field drains and waterproof concrete.[12]

For the mill room we obtained a slate slab billiard and dining table made by E.A. Clarke & Son of Liverpool. This was a lucky purchase from a little house on the Shankill Road. The room is heated by a wood burning stove, which is equipped with a decorative crane.[13] The mill room walls are encased in panelling brought from Purdysburn house. That beautiful old mansion was built in 1825 by Narcissus Batt, founder of the Belfast Bank. The house was demolished in 1960's, to make way for a hospital. Fortunately, I acquired the fine whitepine Purdysburn panelling for preservation at Port Braddan. There was sufficient wood to panel all the walls of the old mill house.

The january connecting the lower and upper floors of the mill house serves the dining room, kitchen, fernery and shower room lavatory. The last is lit by another sidelight from the Titanic store.

The kitchen has a quaint little Georgian fireplace

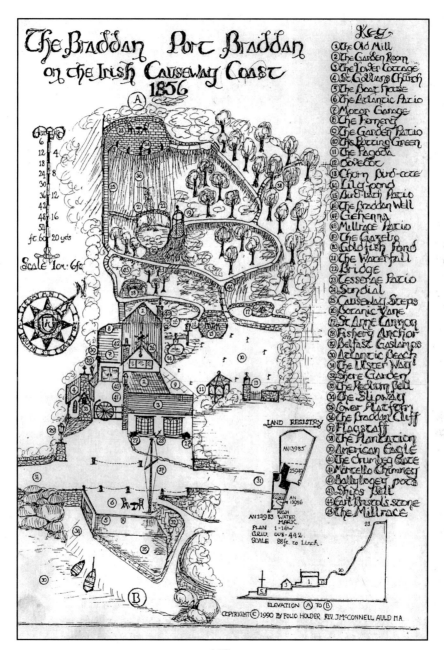

with open hobs, quite capable of cooking a full dinner.[14] The kitchen ceiling rises through the mill house to 28 feet. A staircase climbs to the first storey studio and the area I chose to call *"the ship's bridge"*. It guards the binnacle, a day bed, and a fourth cannon graced by an Enniskillen cannonball.

There is a second wood burning stove in the studio. When all the fires are burning during the Christmas holidays the cottage becomes quite cosy. Chandeliers in the studio were made from hay cart wheels which I found in the coach house, when I bought the property.[15] There is adequate space for various collections of shells, fossils and pictures. The visitor passes through a fifteen paned Georgian door unto the patio.[16]

From the patio a door opens into the garden. The grounds rise about one hundred feet from a sandy beach at the boat house to the cliff top patio. The panorama from the brae-top is spectacular. White Park Bay lies at your feet, Rathlin Island is the focal point, Islay and the Mull of Kintyre float on the horizon. After sunset the sky line twinkles with light houses. The horizon glitters in winter sunshine, when Scotland is snow-bound.

The cliff top patio is paved with bricks salvaged from the demolition of Belfast's first medical school, which was at the Academical Institution.[17] The garden clings to the hill side to make use of an acre of shallow soil. Each year, when I get through the horticultural spring cleaning, I swear one leg is an inch shorter that the other! Many years ago I drew a map to show the pathway around the garden.[18]

A garage was added in due course. It is decorated with an American eagle. Once this proud bird perched on the grand entrance of a great house which was demolished to provide a motorway. Now it nests at Port Braddan for safe keeping.

The story of St Gobban's Church is told by the saint himself in another letter to the mill. The boat house, with its sea-board patio, received planning permission in the early 1970's, before the re-organisation of local government.

The stories behind some of the items in the garden collection will interest you. A pair of military cannon, which decorate the front garden, came from a Dutch sailing ship. She was wrecked off Killough, now the guns guard Port Braddan.[19] The anti-submarine gun beside the boat-house was salvaged from a war ship, which sank in the Irish sea in 1916.[20]

In 1880 the weather vane indicated the direction of the winds which whistle around the trees of Belfast's Botanic Garden. Its original wrought iron base supports the light beside the garage door.[21] A couple of Belfast city street lamps illuminate the pathway to the front door of the cottage.[22]

The ship's bell beside the front door now summons the miller's attention! In 1853 it rang out the watches for the sailors on the good ship *"Galathea"*[23]. Today, with the church bell, it tolls the happiness of those who come to be wed in St. Gobban's Church. The church bell once rang for members of the North Down Hunt as they drank the stirrup cup in Dunvilles Royal Irish whiskey at Redburn in Holywood.[24]. From the same County Down town comes the decorative garden urn atop the fountain of the lily pond. It was made in 1827, for the palace of the Bishop of Down and Connor.[25] A mounting block from Downhill, the sea-side palace of the Earl of Bristol, Bishop of Derry, is another ecclesiastical curiosity preserved for posterity at Port Braddan.[26]

Beside the front door there is a jaunting car

wheel made by P. McCourt of Lisburn. Its twin embellishes the gate. The wheels were donated by one of the many Instonians, without whose hard work 'the Braddan' would not have been built.[27]

When I came to Port Braddan in 1962, I found many broken pieces of grinding stones. They were built into the foundations of various farm sheds which we removed.[28] The pieces were reconstructed into the large circular mill stone which stands beside the garage doors. The gazebo, with its Georgian railings, was built to overlook the waterfall, the cascade of which feeds the goldfish pond.[29] The overflow from the goldfish pond supplies the lily pond in the lower garden.

Formerly all the roofs were beautifully thatched. The three Montgomery brothers of Bushmills were our local thatchers; they taught us the skills of their trade. Only first quality dew retted flax is suitable for making durable roofs beside the salty sea. Our first load of flax came from Castlewellan in County Down. Thousands of stooks filled the garage and the path down to the road, ready to be carried to the roofs.

The hard-working thatchers took six months to complete this very difficult job; the finished effect was very beautiful. Eventually, it became quite impossible to obtain flax, even by import from County Donegal.[30] The roofs had to be re-slated, much to my chagrin. St.. Gobban's Church was the last building to be re-slated. Today only a dove cote in the garden carries traditional Irish flax thatch. I should say the upkeep of a slate roof is indolence

PURDYSBURN HOUSE BUILT BY NARCISSUS BATT ESQ.

165

in comparison with the urgent days of hard work required to repair the winter ravages into the thatch, when the long awaited summer holidays arrived!

It is very difficult to encapsulate within a few pages the rewarding efforts of a hobby which had occupied four decades. Forty years ago, a collector could acquire interesting items at local auctions or by searching the countryside. Seaside properties were still available at reasonable prices, for those who wished to undertake the painstaking restoration required to make them habitable.

Pieces can still be *"picked up for a song"* by those with knowledgeable eyes. A couple of years ago the ancient bell of the Murlough Bay chapel of St Mologue, came to light in Ballycastle. I wish I had been able to acquire it in order to make a campanologists trinity at St Gobban's Church.

There are many Irish cottages, gate lodges and fine old farm houses dotted over the map of North Antrim, which are crying out for tender loving care. If the roof is intact the house can be restored. All the dwellings hold interesting human stories of former families, waiting to be retold. Few hobbies can be more rewarding that seeing your own retreat coming back to life, weekend by weekend. The only disappointment you will experience is when your project is perfected and mere maintenance becomes your forte.

I leave you with a couple of suggestions. Wherever your grappling -iron takes hold, set out to learn the story of the area. I was fortunate to find Port Braddan with ten thousand years of tantalising human geography lying before my front door. Honour those whose home your efforts will revitalize. Please do not tumble the lovely old stone walls, in order to create an anti-environmental concrete erection on the site. You may well save the governmental *'value added tax"* but you will loose the ambience of an old hearth and homestead.

The Greek islands, St Helena and Tristan da Cunha have sacrificed traditional cottages for concrete boxes with tin lids. The Irish countryside is strewn with venerable dwellings. Vacant windows, cold chimneys and silent gardens cry out for industrious weekenders to restore them. If you find such an paragon, I hope you will have as much pleasure as I have enjoyed in transforming an old mill into a comfortable cottage.

"Solum horas solis orientis video".[31]

AUTHORS NOTES

I have made the following inventory for those, like myself, who seek to discover from whence the things around us originate. At sometime in the past, someone must have known the full story of every antique item we possess. Would that *'someone'* had recorded the knowledge for posterity, or *"someone else"* had not incinerated *"all the old papers"* after the death of the owner. This record is for those who may be interested in the items of our heritage. The preceding letter was written to encourage those who have a mind to restore an old property to its former glory. As Irish farms increase in size and farm workers forsake the land, dwellings come available for those who would like to have their own weekend cottage in the country. It is sad to see so many old houses falling into dereliction, when they could be providing sources of enjoyment to industrious weekenders.

1. The pump was acquired from a farm at Mosside. It has a traditional *"Cow's Tail"* pumping handle. I renewed its simple suction mechanism and connected the pipe to the well. Fortunately the mains water supply arrived the following year as families of robins have nested in the pump's water spout every spring since then. The dentated chimney pots (c1840) were salvaged from a school house in the same area. The tall octagonal pot came from Holywood for safe keeping at Port Braddan.

2. I chose to call these four door entry points *"januaries"* from the name of the Roman god Janus who had two faces looking in opposite directions. The first january connects the sitting room, garden room and two cabin-bedrooms. The other connects the dining room, fernery, shower room and kitchen.

3. Originally the mill race was diverted from the Templastragh burn along a wooden sluice to the wheel. Later the machinery was driven by horse power and finally by an internal-combustion engine.

4. Beaconfield Marie Curie Home for cancer care occupies the site.

5. *"Jocelyn Cottage"* was a single storey house set in large grounds on the Woodstock Road in Belfast. The property belonged to my grandfather's family and was developed into Jocelyn Avenue and Jocelyn Gardens.

6. I bought these oversized semi-circular chairs in Ross's Auction Mart in Belfast. When the superfluous upholstery was removed, I discovered fine carved teak frames. The auctioneer informed me that the previous owner had served with the Indian Army in Jaipur; the chairs were a gift from the local Rajah.

AUTHORS NOTES

7. The largest model yacht is *"Fairy Queen"* championship holder of Bangor in the 1880's. *"Gretta"* with red sails was crafted by my father, while voyaging with the Ulster Steamship Company in the 1930's.

8. *"Pretoria Castle"* built by Harland and Wolff for the Union-Castle line. She was broken in the 1930's.

9. During a land drainage project on the Blackwater river, County Armagh, six dug-out boats of fifth century vintage were excavated. Most of these were broken by teenagers for barbecue fires. The smallest boat was sent to Port Braddan for safe keeping. It is 7 feet in length and 1 foot 6ins wide. The hold for a tow rope is still in place and the boat in excellent condition.

10. This item carries the date 1643. The panels and lions' heads with brass rings are original. It was acquired at auction after the Kensington Hotel, College Square East, had ceased to function. It had been part of the fireplace surround in the hotel's reception hall. Possibly it started life as headpiece of a Jacobean bedstead.

11. I found most of the coloured glass net floats on the deserted shores of Rathlin Island. In the 1960's a few were washed up on White Park Bay. The smaller floats were used on Lake Michigan in the U.S.A.

12. For readers who are contemplating conversion of agricultural property for personal use, the complete removal of original floors is essential.

13. Formerly an Irish crane was common to every cottage. Its proper use assured temperature control for cooking and accommodation for pots of every size. There are five cranes in 'The Braddan' one for each fireplace – now purely for decorative purposes. The crane in the dining room came from the public house at *"The Diamond"* County Armagh where the Orange Order was founded in 1795.

14. This delightful item was acquired at auction. It resembles those used in students chambers at Trinity College, University of Dublin. There they provided heat and cooking facilities for undergraduates and a considerable amount of work for the skips.

AUTHORS NOTES

15.   Among other interesting items in the studio are a small naval cannon (see note 27) a George III chest of drawers and a square piano of the same period. (Number 869 by R. Jones & Co of London). The last item compliments the Beckhardt grand in the sitting room.

16.   This beautiful window once graced Drumbeg parish church in County Down. The building was erected in 1795 when plain glass in Y-tracery lancet heads and square panes were the fashion. The window came to Port Braddan for safe keeping in the 1970's. It was replaced by the Uprichard memorial window in Drumbeg church. The Victorian door leading from the patio into the garden also came from St. Patrick's church.

17.   The Belfast Academical institution was founded in 1810 and received its royal accolade from King William IV. It was intended to become a university college and incorporate both theological and medical schools. The morgue and lecture theatre of the medical school remained intact until the 1970's and served as the school steward's carpentry shop. When it was demolished for development improvements some of the bricks were brought to Port Braddan for safe keeping and built into the tessellated pavement of the hill top patio.

18.   The map is printed on an accompanying page.

19.   In a letter dated April 5, 1740, agent Francis Lascelles wrote to his master *Judge Michael Ward,* landowner and trader – *"There is 3 or 4 cannon belonging to a ship lost here I have the selling of them if you have a minde for them will sell at 12 shillings per hundred weight. They are above a pound ball.* Six Cannon had been brought unto the quay at Port St. Anne. Probably the ship came from Holland, bringing military cannon for use in one of the rebellions. In 1965 I acquired two of these important items from the owner of the derelict Port St Anne Harbour at Killough.

20.   The 2 inch bore anti-submarine gun was salvaged by the Cope family of Killough form a ship sunk in the Irish sea during the First World War.

21.   The Stranmillis Road gate lodge to Belfast's Botanic Gardens, (Architect William Batt), was built in 1877 and wantonly demolished in 1965. The clock tower (added 1880 by public subscription) also disappeared in this act of official vandalism. Wing Commander J.S. Higginson acquired the clock. The weather-vane came to Port Braddan for safe keeping.

22.   Although electric lighting had illuminated the Queen's Island pleasure park as early as 1850; it

was not until 1895 that the Belfast City Council built its first generator at Chapel Lane. Even so, it took sixty years to commence the replacement of gas street lighting. By 1964, 11,000 lamps had been replaced. The council hoped to have the scheme completed by 1968. Thousands of the copper gas lanterns became available. I acquired two of the lamps. I connected one to the base of the Botanic Gardens weather vane. This magnificent support had been damaged during demolition of the gate lodge.

23. *"Galathea"* was built in Tvedestrand, Norway, by Messrs. A and F Smith in 1853. *"Galathea"* was wrecked on February 10 1858, at the bar of Youghal, County Cork. She carried 650 tons of guano from Callao, Peru, to Queenstown for orders as to final destination. Watched by 2000 spectators, the lifeboat rescued 16 crew who clambered over the bowsprit to safety. I bought the ship's bell at auction in Belfast (1967) when I required a manual Claxton horn for my MG (B) GT. When I collected the Claxton I discovered I had acquired with it a fine collection of ships' lamps and the bell of *"Galathea"!*

24. Redburn House was designed for R.G. Dunville (Royal Irish Distillery) by Messrs. Lanyon, Lynn and Lanyon in 1867. The property was acquired by the Holywood Urban District Council in 1950 and later demolished. I acquired the great bell from the stable yard tower for safe keeping at Port Braddan.

25. *"Ashfield"* was built by Bishop Mant in 1842 as the diocesan palace. The estate was bought for the British army as the Palace Barracks in 1887 and the great house demolished. Several urns were removed from the palace gardens in 1890 and preserved at Holywood and Port Braddan.

26. The Earl of Bristol, Bishop of Derry built Downhill Castle Co. Londonderry in 1772. This chain pillar was used as a mounting block by visitors to the castle.

27. Many of my former students at the Royal Belfast Academical Institution not only gave their industry, but sometimes interesting items to *"The Braddan"*. A young Instonian, clearing his family's garden at Annadale Avenue, discovered a fine little naval cannon atop a heap of bramble covered stones. We were unable to discover its history. Today it takes pride of place in the studio. Nearby is a First World War hand grenade and a cannon ball used in the battle of Enniskillen (1689).

28. When I bought the property from John McKay, the farm yard had two cart houses, an egg store

as well as the present buildings. The cart houses and egg store were demolished and the land included into the garden. Various shreds of grinding stones were unearthed from the foundation. These were reassembled into the present representation of the mill stone.

29.   The Georgian railings leading to the gazebo came from *"Martello"* in Holywood.

30.   In July 1970 I was able to purchase thatch from Irish Flax Developments Ltd. (Annsborough Castlewellan) at £27 per ton and £18 transport cost for a 5 ton load. The huge Annsborough flax stacks were completely destroyed by terrorist action in the mid 1970's, leaving Northern Ireland without any supply of flax for thatching. By 1979, County Donegal Committee of Agriculture charged £140 for 120 sheaves. Unfortunately Donegal farmers would not allow flax to cross into Northern Ireland. By 1980 it was impossible to obtain flax within the United Kingdom and the three roofs of *"The Braddan"* reverted to slates.

31.   "I see only the hours of a rising sun". (i.e. I am a born optimist). The text inscribed on the tower of St Gobban's church refers to the sundial.

BIBLIOGRAPHY

F ortunately a considerable number of books are available from which to glean the story of Port Braddan and the Causeway Coast. I wish to thank the authors who researched the information for the interest of those who follow. A full bibliography will be found in *"Holywood Then and Now"*.

Adamson, I.	Battle of Moira.	Newtownards 1980
Adamson, I.	Bangor Light of World	Newtownards 1974
Allingham, H.	Narrative of Armada	London, 1897
Ancient Monuments in State Care		HMSO 1966 1
Antrim, A.	The Antrim McDonnells	Belfast 1977
Auld, C.	Holywood Then and Now	Bangor 2002
Auld, C.	Forgotten House of Holywood	Bangor 2003
Bardon, J.	History of Ulster (update)	Belfast 2001
Beckett, J.	Making of Modern Ireland	London 1966
Birmingham, G.A.	Round our North Corner	Ballycastle 1962
Bourke, E.J.	Irish Coast Shipwrecks	Dublin 1994
Briggs, H.	Centenary Diary of N.I.E.	Belfast 1995
Boyd, H.A.	Parish of Ballintoy	Ballymena 1946
Clarke, W.	Rathlin Disputed Island	Portlaw 1971
Connolly, S.J.	Oxford Irish History	Oxford 1998
Cuellar, F.	Adventures in Connacht and Ulster	Antwerp 1589
Dallat, C.	Road to the Glens	Belfast 1989
Dean J.A.K.	Gate Houses of Ulster	Belfast 1991
D.O.E.	Antrim Coast and Glens	Belfast 1988
D.O.E.	Causeway Coast	Belfast 1989
Draper, V.	Children of Dunseverick	Dingle 1994
Dunlop, E (ed)	Recollections of Mary Alice Young	Ballymena 1996
Encarta	World English Dictionary	London 1999
Evans E.E.	Irish Heritage	Dundalk 1942

Evans E.E.	Irish Folk Ways	London 1957
Fedden, R.	Giant's Causeway	London 1971
Flanagan, L.	Wrecks of Armada	Dublin 1995
Hill, G.	Stewarts of Ballintoy	Ballycastle 1876
Hill, G.	Macdonnells of Antrim	Belfast 1873
Kilfeather, T.D.	Graveyard of Armada	Nass 1967
Kirkpatrick, H.	Cataract and its treatment	London 1921
Law, H.T.	Rathlin, Island and Parish	Cookstown 1961
Lewis, A.	Topographical Dictionary	Dublin 1837
Lloyds List	(Youghal) 10.02.1858	London 1858
MacNio Caill, G.	Medieval Annuals	Dublin 1975
McCahan, R.	Local Histories	Coleraine 1988
McDonagh, B. (ed)	Spanish Armada	Sligo 1980
McKay, P.	Ulster Place Names	Belfast 1999
McNamee, E.	The Blue Tango	London 2001
Mason, W.S.	Parochial Survey (Vol I)	Dublin 1814
Mitchel, N.C.	Note on A.McC. May	(U.J.A. 1972) Belfast
Milligan, C.D.	Seige of Londonderry	Belfast 1962
Morton, R.S.	Standard Guage Railways	Belfast 1962
Mullin J.E.	Dunluce Presbyterian Church	Coleraine 1995
Mullin J.E.	The Causeway Coast	Belfast 1974
Newspapers	Coleraine Chronicle	Ballymena
	Observer, Newsletter, Northern Constitution	
	Irish News, etc.	
O'Laverty, J.	Diocese of Down and Conor	Dublin 1880
Ordnance Survey Memoirs	(Antrim)	Q.U.B. Belfast 1994

Praeger, R.L.	The Way That I Went	London 1939
Public Records Office	Causeway Papers	
R.N. Lifeboat, Inst.	The Lifeboat, 01.07.1858	London 1858
Sandford, E.	Discover Northern Ireland	Belfast 1983
School of Tropical Medicine Prospectus		London 2003
Stenuit, R.	Treasures of Armada	Newtownabbot 1972
Stevenson, J.	Life in North Down (1600-1800)	Belfast 1920
Taylor, A.	Carnoustie Panbridge Church	Carnoustie 1990
Taylor, A.	Story of Panbride	Carnoustie 1933

Ulster Architectural Heritage Society.   Glens (1971) North Antrim (1972) Rathlin (1974)

Ulster Journal of Archaeology (Various)

Wallace, B.	Bushmills Presbyterian Church	Coleraine 1996
Warner and Martin	Groundwork of British History	London 1923

INDEX

Most subjects are found easily under the main titles headings in the Contents. However, sometimes rapid reference is required to an item only vaguely remembered by the reader.

INDEX

INDEX

NOTES

NOTES

NOTES